# The VROOMS of the FOOTHILLS

## SINGING A COWBOY SONG

Titles in the Series
# The VROOMS of the FOOTHILLS:

# The VROOMS of the FOOTHILLS

## Volume 5

## SINGING A COWBOY SONG

*Bessie Vroom Ellis*
*and*
*Edith Annand Smithies*

"Time rolled on, as it always does."
~ Memories of Anthony Bruce, Beaver Mines

Order this book online at www.trafford.com
or email orders@trafford.com

Most Trafford titles are also available at major online book retailers.

Print information available on the last page.

ISBN: 978-1-6987-0745-7 (sc)
ISBN: 978-1-6987-0744-0 (hc)
ISBN: 978-1-6987-0746-4 (e)

Trafford rev. 05/20/2021

www.trafford.com
North America & international
toll-free: 844-688-6899 (USA & Canada)
fax: 812 355 4082

In about 1879, Kootenai Brown squatted in this log cabin on part SE31-1-29-4 between Middle Waterton and Knight's Lake in Waterton Park (Map 4). Sheep Mountain (Vimy Ridge) looms in the backmground. This cabin may have been home for Kootenai and his first wife, Olive Lyonnais and their children, and was home with his second wife, Isabella 'Nichemoos'. The cabin stood until the flood of 1908, when a Waterton resident reported seeing the cabin swept downstream through the Dardenelles.

## CONTENTS

# ACKNOWLEDGEMENTS

In the twenty years since I began writing my series *The Vrooms of the Foothhills,* I have had the privielege of interviewing dozens of oldtimers and their families, viewing hundreds of their photos and recording pages of their precious memories. Most of the photos in my book are unique. The originals are of varying age and quality but I want to preserve them in print for future generations.

It's said that, "If you care, you share." So it is with gratitude that I acknowledge the gracious help and valuable contribution made to this, my fifth book, by the following who have shared their photos and memories which might otherwise go unrecorded:

Sonia Chiesa Barclay Anderson, George 'Geordie Annand, Ron Babin, Betty Annand Baker, Art Bell, Marguerite Link Bennett, Nieves Primeau Brister, Harold & Gada Anderson Bruns, Dave Carnell, Brian Carnell, Michael Carnell, Ellen 'Nellie' Dyer Bruce, Katherine Bruce, Jean McEwen Burns, Gladys Charman, Barbara Christiansen, Ed Chrisitansen, Marie 'Mickey' and Effie Christiansen, Frank Cisar, Alvina Bond Clavel, Doug & Sally Bechtel Connelly, Essie McWhirter Cox, Lloyd Cridland, Gladys Cummins, Tom Davidson, Hugh Dempsey, Dr. John Dormaar, Donna Barclay Elliott, Jim English, Bill Gladstone, Frank & Linnea Hagglund Goble, Heather Bruce Grace, George & Kay Kettles Hagglund, Bessie Thomas Halton, Elaine Black Hamilton, Dave Harder, Marvin Harwood, Deb and Maxine Higbee Haug, Jim Hewitt, Edith 'Toots' Jack Hochstein, Lester & Doris Therriault Hochstein, J.C. 'Jack' Holroyd, Tom & Lois Zorn Holt, Greg Howard, Ruby Jaggernath, Tom & Frankie Jenkins, Alma 'Jo' Ballantyne Johnson, Barbara Jones, Verne Kemble, Rod & Nancy Kretz, Robin LaGrandeur, Kathleen 'Kay' McRae, Bill Link, Doug & Lee Gingras McClelland, Elva Ballantyne McClelland, Ryan McClelland, Ina & Mary Lou McDowall, Todd McFarland, Gavin MacKay, Hugh McLaughlin, Anne Pittaway McKenzie, Frances Riviere McWhirter, Larry Mitchell, George & Shirley Scott Mowat, Linda Murphy, Nellie Riviere Murphy, Lindsey Neville, Peter & Pam Niblock, Walter Oczkowski, Dorothy Crook Over, Bertie Jenkins Patriquin, Olga Zurowski Petrone, Lorraine Riviere Pommier, Margaret Hoschka Riviere, Adeline Cyr Robbins, Maxine Pilling Rodgers, John Russell. Sandra Haslam Rothery, BJ Scott, Margerie Warren Shenton, Audrey Walters Shackleton, Jack & Elsie Smith Smith, Bob Thomas, Adam & Hazel Anderson Truitt, Gerald Udal, Bill Walters, Rob Watt and Cal Wellman.

As well, I am grateful to Katherine Bryan, cartographer; Crowsnest Museum & Archives, Coleman; Jane-Ellen Doubt, researcher, Galt Museum and Archives, Lethbridge; Edwin Knox, Resource Management Officer II, Waterton Lakes National Park; Chris Morrison, author; Dr. Peter J. Murphy, Dept. of Forest Science, University of Alberta; Farley Wuth, Curator, Kootenai Brown Pioneer Village Museum & Archives, Pincher Creek; Glenbow Museum and Archives, Calgary; Library & Archives Canada, Ottawa; The Lethbridge Herald; National Archives, Washington, DC; University of Calgary Archives and Special Collections and the US Geological Survey. The support and encouragement of my family cannot be underestimated. If there are people I have missed with my thanks, I apologize for the omission.

# *PROLOGUE*

Homesteaders, settlers and cowboys had their favourite songs, sung around a piano or by campfire light. The chapters and photos in this book speak to some of the well-known songs which resonated down through the years in my Vroom, Tyson and Annand families.

Chapter 1, **Red River Valley**. This was Kootenai Brown's favourite song. Photos in this chapter recount some of the history of his second wife, Nichemoos.

About 1913, at the Brown's house, Lake Linnet, Waterton. (L to R) Back row: Richard Smith, Mary Helene Smith, Eva Smith, Frances Smith, George Gilmore, 'Nichemoos or Blue-Flash-of-Lightning. Front row: Joseph Smith, Joe Ness, Marie Rose Smith, Kootenai Brown, Charley Smith. Glenbow Archives NA-157-1

Chapter 2. **Long Lost Gold Mine in the Sky**. Early oil prospectors and drillers had their dreams of riches. These photos illustrate some of their stories.

Chapter 3. **There's a Church in the Valley**. All Saints Anglican Church, Waterton, was a centre of religious and social life. Jack Holroyd recalled,

"The biggest service I attended at All Saints was in early June 1945, just after victory in Europe had been declared (VE Day). I remember the church being packed; so many just wanted to attend a service to give thanks that the horrible War had ended.

"The main thing about those War Years was pride and patriotism. Everyone tried to help. The women knitted socks and the kids saved pennies to buy a "War Savings Certificate". The kids got a form at the post office, where 25 cents bought a special stamp. With $5.00 worth of stamps, you got a Certificate. It seemed to take ages, but by selling bottles, etc., most kids were able to accumulate a few Certificates.

Waterton, 1941, Geordie Annand on Embarkation leave, and his sister, Betty Baker.

Jack Holroyd continued, "One of my memories as a child is riding my pony to Waterton School on the 7th of May. We'd known for a short while that the War was winding down. We always rode along behind George and Betsy Annand's house across from Lake Linnet. On this morning, Betsy rushed out her back door waving her apron and calling, "the War is over, the War is over". It meant so much to her because her son Geordie was a German prisoner of war. It was the War's end."

Chapter 4, **My Darling Clementine**. When I was a child, the foothills of southwest Alberta were dotted with coal mines. Oldtime prospectors searched for coal, gold and iron. The photos herein tell some of their stories.

Chapter 5, **Make Me a Cowboy Again**. This was a refrain of ranchers and cowboys as urbanization changed the rural landscape forever.

Nettie and George Mowat, married in St. Martin's Anglican Church, Livingstone district, 1928

Chapter 6, **Sweetheart of the Rockies**. Photos and their joyful stories fill this chapter celebrating marriages, anniversaries and old, historic churches.

Chapter 7, **Playing a Cowboy Song**. This book would not be complete without highlighting some of the many musicians, bands and orchestras of southwest Alberta. Dude ranches held weekend dances to which the local people were invited. Dancing to a 2-man orchestra, a fiddle and accordion, provided a stellar memory.

Chapter 8, **Home on the Range**. Through photos and their stories, this chapter salutes the barns which sheltered the ranchers', homesteaders' and settlers' livestock. Without these buildings, large and small, the West could not have been settled.

Chapter 9, **Long Trail A-Winding**. Old trails wound their way through southwest Alberta. They were blazed by the First Nations people, explorers, cowboys, homesteaders, settlers, forest rangers and park wardens. This chapter features photos of both lesser known and well known trails, and the people who used them.

## *RED RIVER VALLEY*

Stories of Kootenai Brown are part fact, part legend. He and his second wife, Nichemoos, have a special place in my family's lore. In 1916, my husband Geordie's parents, Geo. 'Joe' and Betsy Annand, homesteaded the quarter directly west of George Gladstone where Nichemoos lived after Kootenai's death. This led to a family friendship which lasted until Nichemoos' death in 1935. At Kootenai's funeral, Leo Coombs touchingly played Kootenai's favourite song, *Red River Valley*, on a cornet.

About 1863, Kootenai Brown arrived as a prospector at the gold rush on Williams Creek in the Cariboo Country of BC. He had travelled from Europe, via Panama and San Francisco. Shown here about 1864, "Cariboo Brown" moved on to the gold rush on Wild Horse Creek. There he acted as a Special Constable.

In 1865, he rode over the South Kootenay Pass to the Kootenai Lakes (now Waterton Lakes) on his way to Manitoba. He reached Fort Garry in 1866. Kootenai spent many adventurous years in Red River Country and on the western plains of the US. He didn't return to the Kootenai Lakes until the late 1870s. Used with the kind permission of the Pincher Creek and District Historical Society. Accession Number 988.204.2.2A

In 1865, when Kootenai rode out of Pass Creek Valley, he climbed to where he could see Sofa Mtn. He called this the 'Land of Dreams'. This is what he sould have seen from Bellevue Hill, viewing SW across the Badlands and the mouth of Pass Creek the across Middle Kootenai (Waterton) Lake to Sheep Mtn (Vimy Ridge). Credit: M.P. Bridgland 1914/ Geodetic Survey /Library and Archives Canada/e002108114

In 1869, Kootenai married Olive Lyonnais (Olivia D'Lonais), in St. Joseph's Church, Pembina, Dakota Territory on the Red River. This is their granddaughter, Ethel Brown (William) Zamolinski in 1926. Ethel, born in 1906, was the daughter of Kootenai's only son, Leo Brown. Perhaps she bore a resemblance to her beautiful Metis grandmother, Olive. Used with the kind permission of the Pincher Creek & District Historical Society. Accession Number 2002.45.01.

In the spring of 1883, Charles Schoening and Gus Neumann rode from BC over South Kootenay Pass. Very hungry, they came across Kootenai's cabin where Olive fed them. Charles and Gus both homesteaded south of Pincher Creek. (L to R) The Schoening family - Fred, Charles, Jr, Johanna, Ernest, Charles, Sr, (Front) Otto, Dick, about 1897. Used with the kind permission of the Archives of the Pincher Creek & District Historical Society, from "Prairie Grass to Mountain Pass", 1974, page 373.

In 1892, Kootenai was granted his homestead on Part SE31-1-29-4 at the junction of Pass Creek and the Waterton River. This is where he squatted in the late 1870s and ran his Dardenelles trading post and a race track.

Here in July 1969 at Marquis Hole are my son, Jim, and husband, Geordie Annand. Under this spectacular view of Sheep Mtn (Vimy Ridge), Kootenai and his second wife, Isabella 'Nichemoos' lived on their Pass Creek homestead until about 1908. Their hired man was Charles Spence. With tall trees shelterinng their cabin, Joe Cosley described this as an ideal place to keep out the heat of the summer sun and the cold blasts of winter. Their post office was at Oil City in the Oil Creek (Cameron) Valley.

This is Kootenai Brown at an unknown location. He was described as a 'typical western plainsman' with weather-beaten face, piercing blue eyes and long grey hair, which he cut in 1906.

Kootenai was a crack pistol shot who made his own bullets. He gave this bullet mold to his young friend, Delance Strate, who along with Bob Lowe laid Kootenai out the day he died in 1916. Collection of the Galt Museum & Archives P19694684000.5b

About 1960, Theressa and Delance Strate at home in Waterton. Delance knew Kootenai and Nichemoos as early as 1906, when along with his dad, Ad, Uncle Fred and Lu Nielson met Kootenai while rowing through the Dardenelles. Kootenai invited them to a dance at his house. Delance and Theressa were married in 1917 and lived their lives in Waterton. My husband, Geordie Annand, said 'Delance knows more old Waterton history than everyone else combined.'

Inscribed under photo: "*Chee-Pay-Tha-Qua-Ka-Soon* (Blue Flash of Lightning) or Isabella on the Brown homestead about 1892. Kootenai called her "*Neech-e-Moose*" (Cree for Darling). Geordie Annand recalled that Nichemoos kept a spotlessly clean home. Used with the kind permission of the Pincher Creek & District Historical. Accession Number 988.204.01.

About 1895, Marie Louise Spence, Jr. and Samuel 'Lone Man' Johnson. Louise married Billy Gladstone III. Lone Man married Angelique Big Bear. Frances Riviere McWhirter said Marie befriended Nichemoos and spoke Cree to her. Francis remembered, when she was a child in the early 1920s, Lone Man came to the family's Victoria Peak Ranch (Map 5). Her mother, Nellie Gladstone Riviere, fed Lone Man. Frances was scared to death of the old man dressed in ragged buckskin and riding bareback on his Indian pony.

Klem and Johanne Pedersen in 1913. About 1908, his first job was stacking hay for Kootenai Brown in the Park View district. Some of Klem's working companions while building the Pincher-Waterton road were Joedy Bevan, Gus West, Jack Hazzard and Choteau Reed. While Klem was away haying and freighting, Johanne fed the animals, milked the cow, tended the chickens, made the butter and baked their bread. They both knew Nichemoos. Used with the kind permission of the Pincher Creek & District Historical Society, from 'Prairie Grass to Mountain Pass', 1974, page 796.

(Left) 'Granny' Marie Desmarais Gervais. mother of Marie Rose Delorme Smith. Granny's friends and family included other Cree women, including Nichemoos, who came to Mountain Mill and SW Alberta with their families. Many were from Big Bear's camp after the Riel Rebellion. (Right) Bert Riggall in the 1930s. Bert and his wife, Dora, were called by Kootenai to his bedside as he lay dying, but arrived too late.

THIS IS THE LAST WILL AND TESTAMENT of me John George Brown
of Waterton in the Province of Alberta, I hereby revoking
all former Wills at any time heretofore made by me.

I do hereby leave and bequeathe all my real and
personal estate of every description and wheresoever situate
unto my wife Isabella Brown (See-chee-pay-tha-qua-knaeoon)
as her own absolute property.

I do hereby nominate and appoint my son Leo Brown
of Fort McMurray in the said Province of Alberta to be the
Executor of this my WILL.

I desire my said son Leo Brown to take charge of
my said wife and to care for her for the rest of her life.

It is my earnest wish and desire that my remains
shall be buried on the Lake Shore along side my first wife.

I do not desire the attendance of any Clergyman of
any denomination at my funeral in an official capacity.

I desire that immediately after my death the following parties shall be notified of my decease, namely;-

The Theosophical Society, Point Loma, California,
the said Leo Brown and Mr. A.W.Yowel, at Victoria, British
Columbia.

I direct my said Executor to pay all my just debts
and testamentary expenses as soon as he conveniently can
after my decease.

IN WITNESS WHEREOF I have hereunto set my hand
this          20th          day of May, A.D.1916.

SIGNED, PUBLISHED and DECLARED
by the said John George Brown,
Testator as and for his last
Will and Testament in the presence
of us both present at the same
time, who in his presence and at
his request have hereunto sub-
scribed our names as witnesses.

*John George Brown*

*Robert Cooper*
*E.E. Haug*

Kootenai's Will made provisions for Nichemoos' care. Witnesses: R. Cooper, E.E. Haug. Kootenai didn't want clergy officiating at his burial, but Nichemoos had Rev. J.R. Gretton, St. John's Anglican, Pincher Creek, perform the graveside service.

About 1927, (L to R) Marie Rose Delorme Smith and Lena Marie Rose Gervais Tourond. Lena, a widow, was the first wife of Jack T. Gladstone. Some of Lena's children were Bill and Dave 'Vic' Tourond, and Elmire Tourond (Wallace) Gladstone. The women are in front of Jack and Lena's home across from Lake Linnet, Waterton. Both women were friends of Nichemoos. Lena was the midwife for Betty Annand Baker at the birth of her first son, Alfred. Marie Rose and her husband, Charley, founded the Jughandle Ranch locatd northeast of Beauvais Lake. As a widow after 1914, Marie homesteaded SE21-4-30-4 in the Drywood district. Glenbow Archives NA-2539-2.

(L to R) In 1926, Dave 'Vic' Tourond, Les Morrow, 'Chrissie' Christiansen holding Ed, Lillian (Ernie, Sr) Haug, Marjory Tourond, 'Chris' Christiansen and Jack Christiansen (boy). Behind them is Sun Butte Lodge, Waterton Park, built by 'Waddy' Foster, a good friend of my dad, Ralph Vroom. They were all long-time Waterton residents who knew Nichemoos. Ed and Jack were life-long friends of my husband, Geordie Annand.

In the 1940s, Kootenai Brown's homestead cabin on Crooked Creek, just east of the Waterton border SW10-2-29-4. Essie McWhirter Cox said she and her husband, Orville Jr, visited this cabin when it was part of the Ernest Allred ranch. His son, Jim, gave the cabin to the Pincher Creek & District Historical Society. Essies's in-laws, Orville, Sr and Mary Aldridge Cox knew Kootenai and Nichemoos. Mountains in background: (L to R) Crandell (Bear) Mtn, Mt. Blakiston, Bellevue Hill.

Waterton, Alta,
Mar. 21. 1916.

Leo Brown, Esq.,
    Fort McMurray, Alta.,

Dear Leo,-

        Since your last letter my health has been very
bad and it seems only a short time until I will have to
pass in my checks. Never mind about this, it is alright,
a thing we have all got to pass through. When the
thing happens you will be informed by Messrs Thomson &
Jackson, Barristers and Solicitors, Pincher Creek, Alta.,

        When you know this for a certainty I want you to
come here and take charge of my wife Isabella. I am
leaving her what ought to be enough to more than keep
her in shape and help you out for the balance of her life.
I want you to take her up home where you live. She will
be a good help to you in many ways and will be anxious to
join you. If you think it would be better you might live
down here and perhaps be able to make a fair living.
However this is a subject for future consideration.

        Very sorry that I have got nothing but what is
termed bad news, I remain,

                    Your affectionate father, Copy,

Ernie.E. Haug typed this letter dated March 1916 from Kootenai to his son, Leo, asking Leo to move to Waterton to care for Nichemoos.

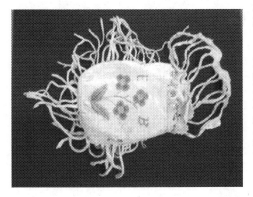

Nichemoos made this fringed white buckskin pouch, with a beaded green flower design in a traditional Cree pattern. It may have carried her medicinal herbs. There are two of Nichemoos' pouches on display at the Kootenai Brown Pioneer Village museum. Used with the kind permission of the Pincher Creek & District Historical. Accession Number 2002.02.03.

July 1916. 'Enroute to the grave site' (of Kootenai Borwn). (L to R) unknown woman; Nichemoos, Isaac Lorin Allred (driver). Nichemoos met Kootenai in 1885, when he was with the Rocky Mountain Rangers in SK. Used with kind permission of the Pincher Creek and District Historical Society. Accession Number 2000.61.3.

Kootenai Brown's funeral cortege heads north enroute to his grave site on the west shore of Knight's Lake. (Left) Sarah Luella Nielson 'Pancake Lou', in white dress, and (right) Bob Lowe, with feet hanging out the back. They are crossing Pass Creek Flats riding on, in Lu's words, 'an Indian wagon'. Betty Annand Baker said that Nichemoos was much younger than Kootenai. Old-time historian, Freda Graham Bundy, referred to Nichemoos as 'a very fine character'. My husband, Geordie Annand, said Nichemoos was very intelligent. Used with the kind permission of the Pincher Creek and District Historical Society. Accession Number 2000.61.2.

George and Betsy, Waterton, summers 1920-1924 on the west side of Pass Creek (Blakiston Brook), at 'lower' Pass Creek bridge. The Annands homestead quarter SE14-4-30-4, Drywood district, had been just west of George Gladstone's quarter. After Kootenai's death, Nichemoos' often lived with Nellie Gladstone Riviere in a little cabin on the George Gladstone place. Geordie Annand recalled that Nichemoos and his mother, Betsy, got along well. His Dad would pick up Nichemoos at Nellie's and Nichemoos would stay for the day with the Annands on Pass Creek. His Dad, George 'Joe', would take Nichemoos down to visit Kootenai's grave.

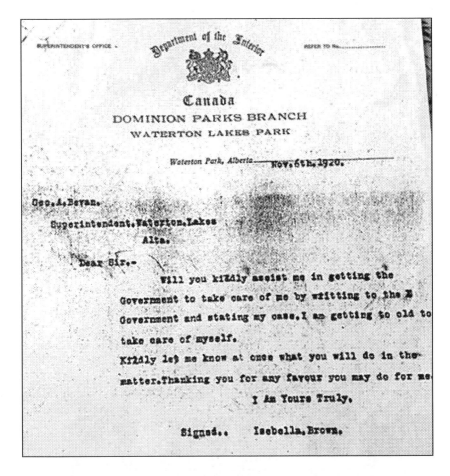

SUPERINTENDENT'S OFFICE .

*Department of the Interior*

REFER TO No.

## Canada
### DOMINION PARKS BRANCH
### WATERTON LAKES PARK

*Waterton Park, Alberta* Nov. 6th, 1920.

Geo. A. Bevan.

Superintendent, Waterton Lakes

Alta.

Dear Sir.-

Will you kindly assist me in getting the Government to take care of me by writting to the Government and stating my case, I am getting to old to take care of myself.

Kindly let me know at once what you will do in the matter. Thanking you for any favour you may do for me.

I Am Yours Truly,

Signed.. Isobella, Brown.

Letter typed by Ernie Haug dated November 1920 from Nichemoos to George Bevan, Superintendent, Waterton Park, asking the Dominion Government to care for her.

On July 1, a Curtis biplane landed on Pass Creek Flats, Waterton, piloted by Palmer and Harry Fitzsimmons. With a shriek of laughter, Nichemoos exclaimed in Cree that it was Kootenai, who had told Canon Middleton that he would return reincarnated in the form of an eagle. Kootenai had been baptized an Anglican but in later years adopted the principles of Theosophy. After each sightseeing flight, Nichemoos excitedly walked around the plane, gently patting and talking to it. Galt Museum and Archives P20151083099.

In the summers after Kootenai died, Nichemoos lived in a tent on Moccasin Flat between Lake Linnet and Aldridge Bay, so as to be near Kootenai's grave. Here in 1923 her tent was clean and neat. Nichemoos called George Baker 'son' because he brought her groceries. Before Nichemoos went to live with Nellie Riviere, Mrs. Malvina Morris, who lived across from Lake Linnet, was paid $20 per month by the Dominion Government to look after her. **Credit:** Parks Canada.

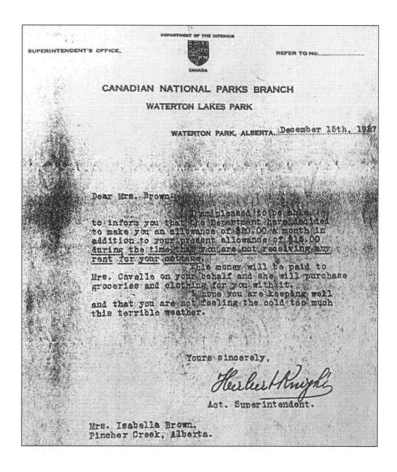

Letter from Bert Knight, Supt. Waterton, Dec. 1927, to Nichemoos that her pension was increased. Payment was made to Flora Clavel (Cavelle) to look after Nichemoos.

After Kootenai's death, Nichemoos lived with friends and in this three room log cabin on Kootenai's Crooked Creek, homestead SW10-2-29-4. In 1918, Joe Cosley, ranger and trapper, stayed with Nichemoos in this cabin after his return from WW1. Joe arrived uninvited and didn't know Kootenai had died. To Joe, Nichemoos appeared "old, emaciated and a physical wreck'. With no social safety net, no children and no immediate family, she had no one to look after her needs and no way to get food since she was too old to hunt. Shown here in 1970, the cabin is being moved to Kootenai Brown Museum in Pincher Creek. (Left background) Bellevue Hill. Used with the kind permission of the Pincher Creek and District Historical Society.

1932 (L to R) Nellie Gladstone Riviere, Nellie 'Babe' Riviere, 'Little' Henri Riviere, at Nellie's home on the George Gladstone homestead, northwest of Twin Butte, AB. (Right of middle) The small log building at middle was Nichemoos' home where Nellie cared for her from the late 1920s until Nichemoos' death in 1935.

View west over George Gladstone's homestead house (left) and barn, SW13-4-30-4, south side of Drywood Cr, George, Sr and Betsy Annand homesteaded SE14-4-30-W4 immediately to west of Gladstone quarter. In background, (L to R) Spread Eagle Mtn. (now Spionkop Ridge) and Drywood Mtn.

In the early 1930s, (L to R) Nichemoos and Nellie Gladstone (Frenchy) Riviere. Nichemoos loved a joke but only allowed close friends to take her photograph. Here she is wearing her customary moccasins; she never wore shoes. The Dominion Government provided a pension for Nellie's care of Nichemoos. Nellie spoke and read to her in Cree.

(Right) 1934, Nichemoos with Nellie Gladstone Riviere, who is holding her grandson, 'Little' Bobby Riviere. Bobby was the first born of Robert, Sr and Mary Burns Riviere. They're standing in the doorway of Nellie's house on her brother George Gladstone's homestead on Drywood Creek. Nichemoos was the 'doctor' for the nearby families. She would take her pouch of herbal medicine and travel by team and buggy to tend to the sick and injured. In the summer of 1934, my Dad and I stayed with Nellie. I met Nichemoos when we kids would take dinner to 'Kookum' Brown in her little cabin. 'Kookum' is a Cree word for Grandmother.

About 1911, Nichemoos' great friend, Margarette Spence holding grandson Jerry Lawrence (Spence) with his brother, Joe, standing beside a pail decorated with a shamrock. Cree women typically made biscuits, not bread.

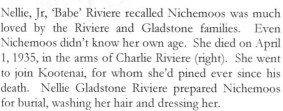

Nellie, Jr, 'Babe' Riviere recalled Nichemoos was much loved by the Riviere and Gladstone families. Even Nichemoos didn't know her own age. She died on April 1, 1935, in the arms of Charlie Riviere (right). She went to join Kootenai, for whom she'd pined ever since his death. Nellie Gladstone Riviere prepared Nichemoos for burial, washing her hair and dressing her.

(L to R) Betsy and George Annand, Sr, at their home on the north shore of Middle Waterton Lake. The Annands were friends and neighbours of Nichemoos since George and his daughter, Betty, had tea with Kootenai and Nichemoos in the summer of 1915.

Driving a team of black horses, on April 3, 1935, Billy Gladstone brought Nichemoos' body through the snow from the Gladstone place out to Hwy 6, where he met George Annand. George drove Nichemoos' body into Waterton in a Parks Department vehicle.

Nichemoos' funeral was held in Precious Blood Roman Catholic Church, Waterton, on April 3, 1935. Father Panhaleux, St. Michael's, Pincher Creek, officiated. As the church was only used in the summer months, it was specially opened for the funeral. Scottie and Clarence Morris had built the church of green logs, with no interior ceiling. Betty Baker said it was like a big, drafty barn on the snowy, bitterly cold, day of the funeral.

Most Park residents attended, including Lillian Haug and Minnie Harwood. Linnea Goble recalled that she, her sister, Esther, and parents, Eric & Olga Hagglund, rode in the back of George Baker's truck to Nichemoos' gravesite on Lower Waterton Lake. Canon Samuel Middleton attended, the Canon being an old and close friend of Kootenai and Nichemoos. Credit Parks Canada.

George and Betty Annand Baker, Waterton, 1943. As a six-year old girl, Betty had tea with Kootenai and Nichemoos in 1915. Nichemoos called George her 'son' because he brought her groceries when she lived in a tent beside Lake Linnet in the summers after Kootenai died. Thomas H. Scott was funeral undertaker. When Tom arrived in Waterton, his hearse had two flat tires. George took the hearse to his Park Transport Garage and repaired the tires so the funeral procession could proceed. As a result, George missed the funeral.

**Pallbearers for Nichemoos.** Ernie Haug, Sr, businessman (above left) and 'Pop' Harwood, postmaster (above right) represented Waterton Park residents.

Pallbearers 'Bo' Holroyd (above left), Park warden, Jack Gladstone, Parks Dept. barn boss, (above right) and Bert Knight, Superintendent, represented the Waterton Parks Department.

Bill Terrill (right) and Fred Bruns of Twin Butte were the pallbearers who represented 'the family and friends of Nichemoos and Kootenai'. Behind Bill is 'the Nunatak' in southeastern BC.

    All seven pallbearers knew Nichemoos from 'the early days'.

# LONG LOST GOLD MINE IN THE SKY

Dreams of untold riches spurred on old-time prospectors. Whether searching for oil, or some other wealth, they imagined life when they 'struck it rich'. An old cowboy song tells of how the happy prospector would be sitting in Heaven, singing, ♫♫ 'Far away, far away. We will find that long lost gold mine some sweet day. And we'll sit up there, and watch the world go by, when we find that long lost gold mine in the sky". ♫♫ Here are some of the stories about the oldtimers' search for oil in southwest Alberta.

Fred Lee (left) was the youngest son of William Samuel Lee. W.S. Lee came into southwest Alberta about 1870, opening a whiskey fort (trading post) 15 miles southwest of Cardston on Lee Creek. He then ranched on the Oldman River at the mouth of Pincher Creek, and finally established a ranch on Lee Lake. Lee began searching for oil and, in 1888, located what he called a "coal oil spring" somewhere near Pincher Creek. This may have been at the later-named 'Kelly's Well', in the Castle River Forest Reserve south of Beaver Mines (Maps 1 & 5).

In about 1886, Chief and Mrs Jacob Bearspaw, Stoneys on their way to Chief Mountain, showed a bottle of oil to perhaps Kootenai Brown or LaFayette French. Here in about 1936 are (4th from left) Roy Marshall, husband of Bertha Ekelund, and (far right) possibly Alvin Ekelund. This photo was taken at Bears Paw cabin, mouth of Blind Canyon, SW21-3-30-4. Ekelund family lore says King Bearspaw is in this photo. King was the grandson of Chief Jacob Bearspaw. King spent his life as a prospector, and searched for the Lost Lemon mine.

In 1890, Joseph Grant came to Waterton from Sarnia via Medicine Hat. Representing Imperial Oil., he drilled a well on SW25-1-3-4, Middle Waterton Lake. Viewing north from the Prince of Wales hill, **"W"** is the location of Grant's 1890 rig just north of Driftwood Beach. **"A"** is the location of Geo & Betsy Annand's home from 1924 to 1945. Grant only drilled through surface gravel before the rig burned down. (Map 4).

William Fernie, William 'LaFayette' French (Smooth Bore), William McArdle and Murray Bellas are among those who drilled to the northeast and east of Waterton, where there were 3 early oil well sites (Map 1) **1**. In 1890, French, Fernie and John Herron of the Southern Alberta Land Co. drilled on Pine Creek, S20-3-29-4 near (later) Oil Trail going from Pincher Creek to Waterton **2**. In 1891, they drilled on Coal Oil Flat, North Yarrow Creek, S34-3-30-4. **3.** In about 1892, they drilled in Coal Oil Basin (Oil Basin), at the head of Cottonwood Creek, S34-2-30-4., in Waterton. We have no photo of French. And, his contributions to early oil drilling are largely unappreciated. By 1901, French owned NW12-8-3-5 in the Lee district. His house burned and he died as a result. French's land was sold to James Milvain. This is the Milvain home on French's quarter.

(Left) The 3rd oil well drilled by LaFayette French and William Fernie's Southern Alberta Land Co. (Maps 1 & 4). Located on S34-2-30-4, now inside Waterton Park, the well's standpipe was for years a marker on the Old North (Stoney Indian, Sundance) Trail, which wound out of Coal Oil Basin over Lakeview Ridge and south to Montana. Previously, in 1891, French and Fernie had drilled on Coal Oil Flat at Smith and South Yarrow Creeks on S34-3-30-4 (Map 1). Using horses with a jig pole, they put a hole down, mostly striking water. Fifty years later, after great expense, the Alberta Gas and Fuel Co. drilled on the same spot and found gas.

During the winter of 1906-1907, John Gloyne hauled, from Columbia Falls and up the North Fork of the Flathead, a steam boiler, oil rig and drilling equipment, food and horses' oats for a year and a sawmill,. They builit a tote road eastward, following the ancient Buffalo (Cow) Trail along Kishenina Creek to the junction with Akamina Brook. (Map 1) Photos above and below are Gloyne's camp about 1920 where Gloyne drilled Akamina #1 (Gloyne's well). Only sulphur water was found in the five drill holes.

In 1907, just below Grizzly Gulch, Gloyne's crew put up a sawmill and buildings. They built a derrick which stood until 1936. Jack Hazzard was a cook for the freighters. When Gloyne's well closed, the steam engine was moved to Jack Hazzard's (later Carl Carlson) Forum Lake mill. Later it was sold to Harvey Bossenberry for his #2 sawmill on West Castle River, south of Beaver Mines. Gloyne, a blaster, was the first foreman in the building of the Akamina Highway to Cameron Lake, 1921-1922.

Pre-1912, this is the Pincher Creek Oil and Refining Co. well drilled on S24-T1-W5 and S25-T1-W5, near Oil City along Lineham Creek. This is a cable tool rig. John Drader formed the company in 1905. Joseph E. Woods, a surveyor and geologist, was a member of the Board of Directors. Drader had been a partner with John Lineham in the Rocky Mountain Development Co, but they had a violent falling out. Drader won a court battle to haul his equipment across RMDC land at Oil City. After drilling to 800 feet, Drader came up dry.There were other old-time oil prospectors in SW Alberta. My dad, Ralph Vroom's, good friend 'Wal' Eddy staked an oil claim on NE14-3-30-W4, which was the NW extent of Cloudy Ridge. As a lad, Wal had prospected for gold with Mr. Garifel along the Bull River beyond St. Eugene Mission, BC.

In 1905, William McDougall Tait became lay minister for the Presbyterian Church at Fishburn, east of Pincher Creek. This is a self-taken flash at the manse. In January 1906, Tait rode from Fishburn to Oil City to hold a prayer meeting. On the way, he visited the Joe Bonertz, Ernest Hillier and Albert Wyckoff families. He also held prayer meetings at the Western Oil & Coal Camp, #3 (Waterton townsite) and WOCC #2 (Cameron Bend). On Tait's return trip, he visited with Kootenai Brown at his homestead SE31-1-29-4 on the Dardenelles of the Waterton River. Tait's guide, Art Thomas, inherited the brand of my great-uncle Thomas Banks 'T.B' Tyson. Used with the kind permission of the Pincher Creek and District Historical Society.

In 1910, Art Thomas is with the 23rd Alberta Rangers (13th CMR in WW1). Bob Thomas told me, "When Oil City was booming, Wm. Tait wanted to go up to hold a meeting with the men but didn't know the way. My uncle, Art Thomas, was just a young guy. Tait got Uncle Art to guide him to Oil City. On their return, they stopped at Hugh & Samantha Glasgow's. The couple each had a gun by their plate. They held a prayer meeting and the old girl broke down and said, 'Well, I guess there's no hope for me'. Folklore recounts that the Glasgows had a US stopping house where they killed people going west from Missouri or Kansas. When people were eating, Mrs. Glasgow would stand behind a curtain, reach out and hit them on the head with a hammer. While near Twin Butte, their children, Joe and Pearl, were taken from them due to neglect.

In 1912, my dad, Ralph Vroom, took this photo of the Rocky Mountain Develoment Co camp at Oil City.. The site was on Oil (Seepage) Creek in the Cameron Creek Valley. Dad was visiting the Sam McVicar family of Beaver Mines who were camping "at the Lakes" for their holiday.

(Left) Looking east in 1919, George Baker took this photo of John Lineham's Discovery Well on Oil (Seepage) Creek in Waterton. In 1985, the well was designated as the first oil well in Western Canada.

(Above right) In 1962, I took this photo of a group at the Discovery Well, Oil City. They are beside a band or bull wheel, used for winching, which still lay at the site.

Cal Wellman told me that in 1941, Del Ellison owed John Wellman money for milk that John had delivered to Del's store in Waterton. Del owned the buildings at Oil City. He repaid John for the 'milk bill' by giving him this original building from Oil City. John and Herman Kenley moved it from Oil City to the Wellman ranch in Park View. They used two teams of horses pulling two wagons side-by-side, upon which the building was balanced. In 2015, this building was still in use on the Wellman ranch. Cal owns Klem Pedersen brand, homesteader and friend of Kootenai Brown.

In August 2015, Bessie Vroom Ellis standing beside the remains of the foundation (lower left) of the never completed, 10-room hotel begun at Oil City, Waterton Park, around 1908. In 1905, a post office opened. People who received mail at Oil City included Kootenai Brown & Nichemoos along with Charles Spence (son of Margarette Spence), Dave Carpenter, John Drader, Maj. Charles W. James NWMP, Foster Hazzard, Jack Hazzard, John Rankin, George Stafford, his father Palmer Stafford, Fred Weiler. Some wives and children lived there, too.

## The Canadian North-West Oil Company, Limited

NON-ASSESSABLE  ——  NON-PERSONAL LIABILITY

### BALANCE SHEET

AT 31st DECEMBER, 1908.

| LIABILITIES | | ASSETS | |
|---|---|---|---|
| Authorised Capital $500,000 in 1,000,000 Shares @ 50c. each | | Property Concession, including Government Fees on Reservation and Title | $196,990.55 |
| Capital paid on shares issued | $360,473.50 | Machinery, Plant and Buildings | 27,592.45 |

In 1907, the Canadian North-West Oil Co, hauled a drilling rig up the Beaver Mines Valley, past my grandfather, Oscar Vroom's homestead NE29-5-2-4. For this Company, in 1907-1910, Jim and Bert Kelly drilled Well #1 and #2 on the West Castle River. Workers who stayed on as settlers included Martin Devine SE28-5-2-5, Alex Dobbie, Andrew O. Hepler SW23-5-2-5 and George Smith, Buckhorn Ranch, NE18-5-2-5.

(Right) My grandmother, Alena Vroom bought shares in the Company. Part of her copy of the 1908 Balance Sheet is shown above.

This 1914 photo shows the well sites of the Canadian North-West Oil Co, taken looking north from Rainy Ridge. The company built a road up the West Castle River and brought in a sawmill from Seatlle. The drilling crew came from Pennsylvania. During the winters, three months' provisions were laid in. Sulphur water flooded into the wells and squelched another hope of a 'gold mine in the sky'.

The top small clearing is on the east side of the West Castle River on NW18-4-3-5. These are Wells #3 & #4, drilled in 1914.

The bottom clearing shows the buildings (bright dots) of the Canadian North-West Oil Co Wells #1 & #2 on the west side of West Castle River on NE7-4-3-5. The wells were located where the trail ascends to Middle Kootenay Pass (Maps 1 & 5). One well was drilled to about 3,000 feet The company was based in Victoria, BC. Credit: M.P. Bridgland 1914/ Geodetic Survey /Library and Archives Canada/ e003900515.

In 1906, Jim and Bert Kelly drilled 20 miles west of Pincher Creek at Kelly's Well and hit gas. (Map 1) This photo, later on the same spot about 1930, was on NE16-5-3-5 just east of the Castlemount Ranger Station, and on the north bank of the Castle River, east of the bridge where the Castle River joins West Castle River. From 1912-1916, when this was part of Waterton Park, Jimmy Miller was the forest ranger. In 1936, as a 9 year-old, my brother Don and I rode our horses to the Bossenberry #1 sawmill at Elk Lodge. We sold raffle tickets to buy Christmas concert presents for Gladstone Valley children. Hazel Truitt (Tourond) was camp cook.

About 1920, 'Mac' or 'Mickey' and Edna McDonald. He had a background in oil well drilling. She was the niece of Peter J. McIlquham, manager of McLaren Ranch at Mountain Mill, and the sister of Ida (Wm) Lees. Edna was a friend of my grandmother, Alena Vroom. In 1911, Mickey was a miner at Beaver Mines and homesteaded NE7-6-2-5.. His land cornered on SW7-6-2-5, homestead of William 'Old Glad' Gladstone. Mount Royal No 1 oil well (Map 1) was on their fenceline.

Dated 1927, Bill Link referred to this as the 'Mac' McDonald oil derrick. Officially, it was the Mount Royal #1 on NE7-6-2-5 at the McDonald-Gladstone fence line southeast of Mountain Mill, east of the creek. In 1929, tools were lost in the hole and it was abandoned by Paul Von Weymarn.

My brother, Don, took me on many adventures. In about 1937, Don and I rode to next the well that Weymarn drilled, in 1929, on the west side of Mill Creek, about one-half mile south of Mountain Mill. Led by one of the drillers, Don and I climbed up to the first platform. It was about 12 feet above the ground with a floor of rough lumber. We looked down at the bottom of the derrick where mud was oozing steadily along the sluice box, also made of rough lumber. Our adventure finished, we mounted our ponies and rode home. We always made sure that we got home before dark.

In 1928, Imperial Oil #1 on the Bob Hedderick place, also known as the Riviere place, on Drywood Creek, west of Hwy 6. This massive wooden derrick used walking beam drilling. The drill was connected to a large cable, powered by a steam engine, making the drill pound away. Background (L to R) Spread Eagle Mtn and Spinokop Peak, Drywood Mtn, Pincher Ridge (above derrick), and Victoria Peak (Map 5).

About 1934, daughters of Jack and Laila Bechtel having 'tea' at their playhouse. (L to R) Jacqueline with her doll, Nona and Inga. The small bulding was moved from the Alberta Gas & Fuel well on Coal Oil Flat from about 1920-1934. It was near their parent's home quarter SW35-29-3-4.

In 1985, sisters Nona Bonertz and Jacqueline Therriault at the site of the Alberta Gas and Fuel well at the junction of North Yarrow and Yarrow Creeks in the middle of Coal Oil Flat NE34-3-29-4 (Map 1). Only this stone fireplace remained. With no modern geological technology, Lafayette French, with horse power, put down a jig pole rig on this same spot 100 years earlier.

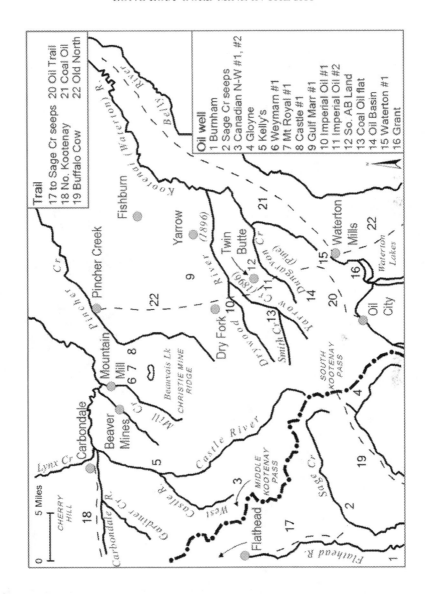

**MAP 1   OIL WELLS & TRAILS, SW ALBERTA and SE BC, circa 1875-1940**
**Oil well:** Alberta Gas and Fuel Co (Lunn-Castle #1), Yarrow-Coal Oil Flat, Waterton-Jenkins #1), Burnham, Canadian North-West Oil #1, #2, #3 and #4, Gloyne, Grant, Gulf Canada Marr #1, Imperial Oil #1, Imperial Oil #2 (Frank Allred), Kelly's, Mount Royal #1, Oil Basin, Oil City (Waterton Park), Sage Creek, Southern Alberta Land Development Co (Imperial Oil #1), Weymarn Oils #1 **Trail:** Buffalo (Cow), Coal Oil, Oil Trail, Old North (Sundance, Stoney Indain), trail to Sage Creek seeps **Post office:** Beaver Mines, Dry Fork, Fishburn, Mountain Mill, Oil Ctiy, Waterton Mills, Yarrow **Townsite:** Carbondale, Flathead

In about 1905, (L to R) Mary Aldridge and her mother, Annie (Bill) Aldridge. Women and children were among the unsung workers who made early oil exploration possible. Annie raised 13 children while living in Waterton and at Oil City. Often, she was extremely isolated; food was scarce with the occasional bear and lots of fish, boiled or fried, to feed her large family. She nursed men taken ill with mumps at Oil City.

In 1916, (L to R) Marjie, Essie and Bill McWhirter on the family's cow 'Skinny'. In the early 1930s, Marjie and Anna Anderson cooked at the Alberta Gas and Fuel Co. oil well at North Yarrow (Smith) and South Yarrow Creeks on Coal Oil Flat NE34-3-29-4. (Map 1). Marjie helped Laila Bechtel, who lived on a nearby homestead, when Jacqueline was a baby.

In 1910, Emma and Walter Cridland. With a multi-horse team, in about 1901, Walter freighted the pipe from Pincher City to Lineham's 'Discovery' Oil Well. About 1904, Klem Pedersen freighted boilers over the Badlands and the steep Blue Lake Trail to the nearby Western Oil and Coal Co. well at Bill Aldridge's site on Oil (Cameron) Creek.

Here in 1933, Jimmy was the son of Alex and Mary Burns. Alex was a teamster who freighted to the wells on Oil (Cameron) Creek, Waterton.

At the time, Clarence Snyder was a driller at Oil City and helped build corduroy roads for access. Clarence married Elsie Dobbie, who he met at Oil City. Elsie was the daughter of William Dobbie whose 'Dobbie freighters' hauled a lot of equipement to the sites. In 1906, Alex Dobbie was the foreman of the 'Oil Camp Gang' at the Canadian Northwest Oil Co well on the West Castle River.

This is the casing of an orphan well drilled by the Magnet Oil Co in 1914 on SE4-8-2-5 (Robert H. Burn and Baxter place), northwest of Lundbreck. It went down over 1000 feet. The casing rises 8 in. and is 12 in. across. The fencepost warns of the hazzard. In 1914, Bert Connelly hauled lumber to the site. About 1930, Ralph Gold was a driller. Elsie Stewart, who cooked for the crew, married Ralph in 1932. In the 1940s, Bill Torrence was a night watchman at the site.

About 1955, Burnham Creek oil derrick at the bridge just west of the Flathead River near the US border (Map 1). (L to R) Delton and Ken Smith, brothers of Jack, of the Spread Eagle district. Charlie Wise was the caretaker. Like many derricks, this was partially built of equipment and materials from abandoned wells, in this case from Akamina #2 at the site of Gloyne's wells, west of Cameron Lake (Map 4).

In 1950, (L to R) Dave Harder, Bruce Bohne, Bill Vroom and Bob Sharp in the log bunkhouse they shared at the Buckhorn Ranch, Gladstone Valley (Map 5). Dave, Bruce and Bill had the same waist size and leg length so first up in the morning was the 'best dressed' for the day!

Dave said, in the early 1930s, Bob carried 1000 feet of drill cable by mule train from the Weymarn derrick south of Mountain Mill to the (British) Columbia Oils wells on Sage Creek, east of the mid-Flathead Valley (Map 1). The continuous cable was looped around the mules' pack saddles. Bob's packtrain went west up the Carbondale River, over the North Kootenay Pass, then south past the Flathead townsite. This was surveyed in the 1920s in anticipation of an oil boom that never materialized. The trail then wound south, down the Flathead River to Butt's ranger station, then east up Sage Creek to the 'seeps'.

(Right) About 1950, Gulf Canada No. 1 Marr well (SE29-4-29-4) on Frank and Inga Marr ranch. The steel derrick was built in the late '40s or early 50s on the west end of Marr Lake. (Left) Marr School on NW21-4-29-4. (Background L to R) Loaf Mtn, Drywood Mtn, Castle (Windsor) Mtn, Victoria Peak, Corner Mtn (Maps 1 & 5).

Tom Jenkins said there was a 'scam' well built on S27-2-29-4 about 1914 and drilled to 35-40 ft. His dad, Walt Jenkins, said the promoters had no intention of drilling for oil; it was just a ruse to get money from investors.

Dated July 1928, this is the collapsed derrick of Alberta Gas and Fuel Co Waterton #1 well on the Jenkin's ranch S34-2-29-4, west of the Waterton River. Scottie Morris and his wife, 'Wes', worked at this well (Map 1).NA-138-2 Glenbow Archives, Special Collections, University of Calgary.

In 1921, Imperial Oil Twin Butte #2 well, Frank Allred homestead SE20-3-29-4 (house right of centre) on Pine Creek (Map 1). Drillers were Clarence Snyder, Bill Videan. Workers were Jim Dobbie, Jim Foote, Red Harrison, Slim McLean, Ernie Saunders. Cooks were Mrs. Norman Chaput, Mrs. Krause and son Ellis, and Joe Whittaker. The well was drilled with a cable tool rig and gas engine to a Canadaian record 4400 ft. It hit gas, but no oil, and lasted two years. Photo by S.A. Harwood from the Ekelund place.

# THERE'S A CHURCH IN THE VALLEY

♫♫ There's a church in the valley in the wildwood, no lovelier place in the vale.
No spot is so dear to my childhood,
As the little brown church in the dale. ♫♫

Early settlers and cowboys were dependent on the weather, and the health of themselves, their animals and their crops. They were of many religions, having been raised in families who attended church regularly. When they settled new districts, they had services in homes and eventually worked together to build churches. This chapter tells the story of one such church, All Saints Anglican, Waterton Park, AB.

About 1907, the Harrad family on their Starlight Ranch S12-7-29-4, on Pincher Creek.. (Left) Charles, Percy (in door), unknown, Hilda, Elizabeth, aunt of Sam Middleton. After some years as a cowboy near Brocket, AB, Sam became an Anglican minister and founded All Saints Church, Waterton. Used with the kind permission of the Pincher Creek and District Historical Society, Prairie Grass to Mountain Pass, 1974 ed, p. 58.

Sam Middleton familiarly known as 'Canon', recalled that Emery LaGrandeur (here in about 1900) saw him thrown from 'Billy', Sam's Peigan cayuse. "Don't let a western cayuse cause you to be a sky pilot", said Emery.

The erratic but faithful 'Billy' carried Sam to Waterton in 1905, where he met Kootenai Brown, called 'Inuspi' by the Blackfeet for his long, flowing hair. It was the beginning of Sam's decades-long dedication to Waterton and All Saints Church. The 'Canon' was the little church's longest serving clergy.

About 1911, William McDougall Tait, a lay minister of the Presbyterian Church. He covered the wide area of Fishburn-Robert Kerr-Waterton. It's said he rode over 10,000 miles around his Mission. In 1906, he ministered to crews at Oil City and Waterton town. Kootenai Brown's diary records "Parson called today", January 17, 1906. Tait meticulously recorded Kootenai's stories in a book "I Remember".

Middleton and Tait likely met when Middleton, in 1909, became headmaster, St. Paul's School, Blood Reserve, on Big Island in the Belly River, near the old whiskey fort of Slideout. Credit: Used with the kind permission of the Pincher Creek and District Historical Society.

The majesty of Waterton, about 1919. (L to R) Jack Hazzard's tourist tent camp and Hotel, and boat docks; Dewitt Johnson Garage (later the Palace Dance Hall). Ernie Haug, Sr, had a place for meals. Those who visited took tents and stayed for a few days, mainly fishing. Summer and winter, 1910-1928, 'Canon' Middleton held Anglican services variously from the back of a wagon on the lakeshore, in the Hotel dining room, on the mountainside under the pines, and in cottages.

Betty Annand Baker recalled that Mabel Dilatush, first wife of Nahor, was a main proponent for the building of All Saints. In 1915, 'Canon' Middleton (left in about 1920) applied to Supt. Robert Cooper for leases for All Saints and a church cottage. Canon's idea that the church buy and move Jack Hazzard's old dance pavilion came to nothing. But, in 1917, a permit was fianlly issed for a Church on Lot 9-Blk 4 and cottages on Lots 5-6-7-Blk 5.

Middleton was a friend of Kootenai Brown, who was an Anglican by baptism and a Theosophist in later years. Kootenai hoped he would be reincarnated as an eagle. Kootenai, a learned man, and Middleton discussed many scientific and literary subjects.

These men, who served in WW1, and their families were members of All Saints Church. In 1933, (L to R) Jack Giddie, Waterton River warden, 'Bo' Holroyd, 'Mac' McAllister, Pass Creek warden, Bert Barnes, Belly River district warden.

Other men who served in WW1, and whose families were parishoners of All Saints, were (above left) 'Chris' Christiansen, in about 1952, with wife 'Chrissie' at Pass Creek district warden cabin. (Above right) In 1943, Jack Pittaway, Sr., in Waterton.

(Above left) Leonard Zorn with wife, Mildred, in the 1960s, Waterton. They and their four daughters (Doris, ElsieAlice, Lois) were active All Saints parishoners from the 1930s – 1970s. (Above right) About 1948, Joe and Emma English, with grandson Jimmy English, were members of All Saints. They're at their home across from Lake Linnet which was originally built by Jack Gladstone son of pioneer William 'Old Glad' Gladstone. Leonard Zorn and Joe English served in WW1.

Middleton's dream was realized on July 1, 1928. The official opening was held for All Saints, Waterton's first church. Many contributed to the Church Building Fund. Louis Hill, President, Great Northern Railway, made a substantial donation to his so-named 'jewel'. The Anglican Women's Guild sold embroidery and the men contributed their labour. **Credit:** Parks Canada.

(Above left) About 1960, (L to R) Doug Oland, Sr, and James Scott. Contractors Oland & Scott built the Prince of Wales Hotel and All Saints Anglican. Scott was a member of the Anglican Church. (Above right) In 1957, 'Pop' Harwood and his son, Steve. The Harwood family were very instrumental in All Saints Church from its inception. Pop was a great friend of Kootenai Brown.

The Gregory family was active in All Saints from the 1920s to the early 1950s. (Left) Nellie (Percy) Gregory and I were members of the Women's Auxilary for many years. Nellie played the old pump organ and often oversaw Sunday School. In 1948, she played at my wedding, accompanying my new sister-in-law, Betty Annand Baker, who sang "I Love You Truly".

Other members of the All Saints WA at the time included Sophie Allison, Vera Ayris, Effie Black, Nellie Giddie, Marjorie Harwood, Jean Haslam, Betty Meads, Lily Middleton, Sybil Reeves, Aileen Rhodes and Mildred Zorn. I took piano lessons when my children were young , in part to play the organ at All Saints when Nellie Gregory could no longer do so after 1950 when she broke her hip while at a WA district meeting in Blairmore.

About 1953, (L to R) 'Paddy' Cousins, Shirley, Martha and Vern Albiston, and Effie Black. Effie, and her mother Ellen Barnes, were members of All Saints. Martha was the daughter of Billy McEwen. Billy was born in 1882. His father, Peter, was an original member of the NWMP. Billy gave up legal studies to be a cowboy. He worked for the Walrond Ranch and many other outfits. As a member of All Saints, his funeral service was held in All Saints in December 1963. He's buried in Waterton cemetery.

About 1960, cairn on Main Street, Waterton, dedicated in 1936 to the memory of Kootenai Brown. The committee included Canon Middleton, 'Pop' Harwood, Ernie Haug, Sr, and Russell Bennett. Bert Pittaway helped 'Pop' build the cairn. The All Saints Church massed choir sang hymns at the ceremony. The plaque, made at Anaconda, MT, reads in part:, FRONTIERSMAN, PIONEER, GENTLEMAN. ARRIVED AT WATERTON LAKES IN 1868. FIRST SUPERINTENDENT OF WATERTON PARK 1910-1914. BORN IN ENGLAND OCT 10, 1839. DIED AT WATERTON JULY 6, 1916. ERECTED BY HIS FRINEDS OF PIONEER DAYS.

1933, Waterton Ladies Sewing Circle at Betty Annand Baker's home, Evergreen Ave. (Clockwise L to R) 'Lettie' Goble (far left, white hat), Annie Eddy Morris, (white hat) Agnes Ford**, unknown (black fur collar), Inez Stratton (standing), Minnie Harwood** (standing), unknown (seated), Hannah Presley (adjusting glasses), Jean Galbraith**, Olga Hagglund (partially obscured, striped coat), Nellie Hunter Goble** (seated, turning to face camera; later Mrs. Gerry Hadfield), 'Chrissie' McKenzie Christiansen** (back to camera). ** Denotes members of All Saints Women's Guild.

Until its demise, in July 2014, two illuminated manuscripts hung in All Saints listing names of Waterton residents who served in WW2. Photos of some are on these two pages.

(Left) July 1941, on enlistment, (L to R) Geordie Annand and Bert Pittaway at the Calgary Stampede.

1944 in Waterton, (L to R) Kevin Goble, Jack Holroyd, Alton 'Hoot' Carlson. Kevin, son of Oliver and Arletta, and 'Hoot', son of Carl and Ada, were home on a short leave from basic training, soon after they joined the Canadian Army.

(Left) Jack Christiansen, in 1945. From 1947-1952, Jack was a warden, with his wife Effie and three young daughters, in the very remote Mt. Robson and Rocky Forks districts of Jasper NP. In 1952, Jack was transferred to Waterton, where he had grown up. The MacKenzie family of Jack's mother, Chrissie, were friends of the Annand family at Caldwell, AB, from 1913.

(Above right) About 1940, Betty Gregory, CAE, and her twin brother Bill Gregory, RCAF (left). In the 1920s, their parents sold their ranch near Twin Butte to Bill and Elsie Baker, parents of George Baker, and moved to Waterton.

(Right) About 1941, Donald 'Bud' Morris, Royal Canadian Navy, son of Cliff Morris. Bud was a best friend of my brother, Don Vroom, when we attended Waterton School 1940-1941.

John 'Peg Leg' and Malvina Morris, and sons Scottie, Cliff, Gene, Bill and Clarence moved to Waterton about 1919 from the Ashvale district NE of Cowley, where they were rabchubg neighbours of Nahor and Mabel Dilatush (later of the Tourist Café, Waterton). The Morris family had the saddlehorse rental outfit at Park headquarters, across from Lake Linnet, in the 1920s and 1930's.

(Left) In 1940, Ralph Vroom, Royal Canadian Artillery, Calgary, AB. Dad also enlisted in WW1.

(Right) Fall 1949, Levi Ashman, licensed BC guide. Levi was in the CV Guard (Veterans Guard of Canada) in WW2. He also served in WW1. In 1926, Levi, a Welsh coal miner, began trapping with Charlie Wise in southeast BC.

About 1935, (L to R) Carnell brothers Bill, Pat, Charles, and Jack holding Jimmy, son of Charles. In WW2, Bill, US Army, helped build the Alaska Hwy. Raymond (not shown) was a cook. Their sisters, Jean (above right) was in the US Army Nurse Corps; Ethel, a long-time Waterton resident, was in the Royal Canadian Corps of Signals.

In 1945, after the end of WW2, (L to R) Calvin, Enid, John (father), Harry, Rhoda (mother, in front of Harry), Jennie, Elaine and Bill Wellman. Harry (Royal Canadian Artillery) and his father, John (RCAF), had just been demobilized and returned home to the family's Waterton Ranch, Park View district, on Sec 30-2-29-4.

All Saints was an integral part of Waterton. In July 1942, there was a glimmer of hope in the dark days of WW2 when two flags were donated to All Saints. Americans in uniform and Waterton residents crowded the wild-flower decorated church and nave. In a friendship ceremony, Robert Hunt, on behalf of Carl Hummer and Christ Episcopal Church, Kalispell, donated the US Stars & Stripes. Joe Bull Shields, on behalf of St. Paul's Anglican, Cardston, donated the Canadian Union Jack. Glenbow Archives NA-3910-64.

Christening of Gladys May Cameronian Foster conducted by Canon S. Middleton, Cameron Lake, on August 8, 1931. (L to R) Elenora Hunter, Walter 'Waddy' Foster holding Gladys, Eda Foster, Canon Middleton, 'Pop' Harwood (godfather), Sophie Middleton (Allison), godmother. Glenbow Archives NA-3910-87.

About 1940, All Saints choir in front of the church. (L to R) Back row: Unknown, Elsie Zorn, Mildred 'Sis' Christiansen, Alice Zorn, Gerry Bailey, unknown. Front row: Mrs. Francis R.K. Hewlett, Isabel Udll, Canon Samuel H. Middleton (seated), Vera Ayris , Betty Giddie, Helen Gregory.

About 1950, 'Slim' and June Udal on Emerald Bay, Waterton. Slim operated the tour boat 'Miss Waterton'. He died in a boating accident just prior to the 1958 Waterton Days. His funeral was conducted by Rev. R.A. Burdon at All Saints. 'Slim' is buried in the Waterton cemetery.

About 1940, Billy McEwen in the yard of 'Slim' Wacher across from Lake Linnet. Slim was a pallbearer at Billy's funeral at All Saints, Dec. 17, 1963. Billy was an old-time cowboy, teamster, and storyteller. He was the son of original NWMP, Pete and Mary Gladstone McEwen - she was the daughter of 'Old Glad'. Billy and Annie McEwen had one daughter, Martha Albiston of Waterton. Billy was the first guest Geordie Annand and I invited to dinner after we were first married in 1948. Credit Art Bell.

Sunday, October 20, 1940. Confirmation of young people into the Anglican Church of Canada, All Saints Church, Waterton. (Left to right) **Back Row:** Lucille 'Susse' Carlson, Isabel Udell, Gerry Bailey, Doris Zorn, Elsie Zorn, Nan Delany, 'Kay' Rackette, Dorothy Udell, Canon Samuel H. Middleton **Seated:** Bishop Louis 'Ralph' Sherman, Archdiocese of Calgary **Kneeling:** Alton 'Hoot' Carlson

September 27, 1945 after the marriage of Ernie and Elsie in All Saints Church. (L to R) Leonard and Mildred Zorn, Ernie Cridland, Elsie Zorn, Emma and Walter Cridland. The Zorns moved to Waterton in the 1930s. Leonard was the park's electrician. They and their daughters Doris, Elsie, Alice and Lois were members of All Saints. Emma was the daughter of pioneers Moise and Julia LaGrandeur. Walter had been a teamster freighting boilers for the building of the Prince of Wales Hotel.

(Left) In 1949, Carl and Lucille Carlson walking down the aisle of All Saints. Canon Middleton officiated at 'Susse's' wedding. Guests included oldtimers Lillian Haug, Annie Lane., Ada Campbell and Isabella Joyce. In the 1930's, Carl had a sawmill near Forum Lake in the Akamina Creek Valley. It was ¼ mile uphill from Levi Ashman's cabin which was built in 1921 by Ernie Haug and Bill Nixon.

(Above right) About 1950 (L to R) Carl Carlson and Jack Giddie, Waterton. Carl's funeral was in All Saints, June 1973. Pallbearers were Gerald Hadfield, Ernie Haug, Jr, Gunmar Holte, Lee Lerner, Stuart Sandford and Delance Strate. Workers at Carl's sawmill included Delance, Orville Cox, Ken Goble and Jonny Eklund. Jack, a Waterton Park warden, was a long-time vestryman for All Saints. In 1909, Jack was the packer for Charles Walcott, of the Smithsonian, to the Burgess Shale fossil beds in Yoho NP. Giddie Creek was named for Jack while he was a Yoho district warden.

## *MY DARLING CLEMENTINE*

♫♫ Oh, my darling, oh, my darling,
Oh, my darling, Clementine.
You are lost and gone forever,
Dreadful sorry, Clementine. ♫♫

When I was a child, small mines dotted SW Alberta. Discovered by old prospectors, ranchers and others, here are the stories of some of these mines.

In 1904, (L to R) Kootenai Brown and Jack Simons, friends of Jack Street. Jack Street joined the NWMP as Reg. No. 596. About 1905, Street had a placer (gold) mine on Street Creek, Glacier NP, on the east side of Upper Waterton Lake. Street died in 1912, while hunting goats with Kootenai, when he plunged off a snow cornice from Goat Haunt Mtn into the small lake below. He was buried beside the lake. Later, about 1930, Jack Hazzard found gold in Grizzly Gulch (Map 4) and started a 'gold rush' in the Akamina Valley, BC. Used with the kind permission of the Pincher Creek and District Historical Society. Accession Number 990.53.

1881, the crude entrance of a mine. Early mines were prone to collapse if the wooden props weren't installed correctly. This was the first coal mine operated at (later) Lethbridge by Nicholas Sheran. He came west as a whiskey trader. Once the NWMP shut down trading whiskey to the Blackfoot, Sheran turned to coal mining. NA-1948-2 Glenbow Archives, Archives and Special Collections, University of Calgary.

About 1913, Jack Hazzard prospected and developed a coal mine on Lakeview Ridge, Sec 30-2-30-4. **"X"** marks its location. Bert Riggall helped work it. Pat Carnell, Jr, recalled as a youth finding the abandoned mine and a box of dynamite. It had a tunnel with a short rail track to push out cars of coal. The coal was of poor quality.

(Above left) Jack Hazzard. Used with the kind permission of the Pincher Creek and District Historical Society. (Above right) In 1919, the original Discovery Well No. 1 at Oil City, as photographed by George Baker. Jack used the lodgepole pine burned by fire as props for his Lakeview Ridge coal mine (Map 4).

In this view SW from Lakeveiw Ridge to Upper Waterton Lake, **"X"** is the location of a coal mine (Map 4) on South 24-2-30-4, east side of Trail (Galwey) Creek, operated 1927-1928 by the Morris brothers of Waterton (Scottie, Cliff, Gene, Billy, Clarence). Father, John 'Peg Leg', had coal mines SW of Pincher Creek on 16-6-30-4 (1911-1913) and 'Black Diamond' in Lundbreck on NE14-26-7-4 (1915-1917). Credit: M.P. Bridgland 1914/ Geodetic Survey /Library and Archives Canada/e002107411

Waterton about 1940. (L to R, back row) MacLean's Waterton Dance Pavilion (partial), Dilatush's Stanley Hotel, butcher shop, old Lorin Allred home, Carlson home, RCMP office. (L to R, front row) Haug's garage, a food market, Delany's Grocery Store, Brewerton Movie Theatre and (far right) Crystal Simming Pool built by Allred. The pool operated from 1924 to the late 1940s. Locally mined coal had many uses. In the 1920s, Oaklie Thompson hauled coal from a mine on the Beazer Ridges to fuel the furnace that heated the pool water.

In 1947 Linnea & Frank Goble at Charlie Wise's cabin (built of old-growth larch) on Nettie Creek, southeast BC. In 1910 Charlie had a homestead on the Flathead River at the Canadian border (Map 1) near where he had a placer gold operation. He was a friend of Kootenai Brown, Jack Street, Chaunce Beebe, Joe Cosley and Levi Ashman.

About 1920, Nels Eric Ekelund beside the entrance to his copper mine on Coppermine Creek, Waterton (Map 1). The mine's location was upstream from the Coppermine Cr picnic shelter in 2016. Jack Holroyd recalled that, in the 1930s, there were remains of a shaft, about 4 feet deep, and signs of digging. However, there were no signs of the mine by 2016.

Nels was a Swedish oldtimer who brought his family from Utah to homestead NE 20 & NE28-2-29-4 in Park View district. Nels was very skilled with an axe and built many log residences that are still used in Waterton in 2021. His son, Junius, while a Park warden at Yarrow Creek, blazed the trail from Oil Basin to the head of Trail Creek and also helped build the first bridge over the Waterton River at the Park entrance.

Anaconda copper (strip) mine, Butte, MT, in about 1930. Men from the Beaver Mines district and Waterton came here to work in the early '30s. W.D. McDowall ran a business in Butte. Cliff Lang, Cal Hunter, Ken McDowall, Harold Vroom and son, Oscar Vroom Jr worked in the mines. Sadly, in 1932, Oscar, at 19 years, died of appendicitis in Butte, never to see his mother again.

About 1905, on Iron Mine Flat, Dungarvan (Pine) Creek, Sec 12-3-30-4, mines were operated by William Dobbie on NE, Billy Huddlestun on SE and Buddy Jamieson on SW quarters. View west (L to R) Lakeview Ridge, Dungarvan Mtn 'The Horn', Spread Eagle Mtn, Victoria Peak, Drywood Mtn, Pincher Ridge and Corner Mtn (in distance).

'Buddy' Jamieson's cabin on SW12-3-30-4 where he staked an iron (magnetite) claim in about 1905. (L to R) Dungarvan Mtn and Spread Eagle Mtn.

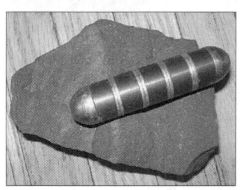

This is a magnet made from magnetite rock of the type found on Iron Mine Flat Sec 12-3-30-4. When grazing, cattle can eat nails, wire or other sharp, metallic objects. A magnet is fed to cattle to collect such objects in their stomachs which may cause 'hardware' disease. In 2010, Dr. John Dormaar of the University of Lethbridge confirmed the presence of a band of magnetite in the side of Dungarvan Creek.

View south across the Carbondale River (Railway River), the north border of Waterton NP 1914-1921. Carbondale townsite is to right of photo (Map 5). There about 1900-1920, Carbon Hill Coke & Coal Co. and Head Syndicate Ltd. had coal mines. Credit M.P. Bridgland 1914/Geodetic Survey/Library and Archives Canada/e004414320.

About 1910, view south to Carbondale Hill from Scotty Wells' homestead NE9-6-3-5 (Map 5). He was on the last big roundup at the Walrond Ranch and 'worked out' in the coal mine at Carbondale to make extra money while homesteading. His daughter, Irene, married Bill Picard, Sr, of Beaver Mines. Credit Crowsnest Museum & Archives, Crowsnest and Its People, page 891.

Viewing east, in 2014, Bessie Vroom Ellis is on the west side of Carbondale Falls on the Carbondale (Railway) River. The old Carbondale townsite is left of photo on SE 12-6-4-5 (Maps 1 & 5).

The Lynx Creek ranger cabin on the north bank of the Carbondale River. Viewing west, Cherry Hill is behind and Lynx Creek is to the right. This was near Andy Bower's homestead which was just north of Carbondale townsite (Map 5). Andy, his wife and family lived in Beaver Mines from about 1915-1925. Daughter, Cathie, taught 1939-1940 at the 'Chicken Coop' School on Uncle Harold Vroom's ranch SE 32-5-2-5 in the Beaver (Mines) Creek Valley. Andy was a NWMP, forest ranger and Waterton warden. Photo by A. Knechtel, 1911. Dominion Forestry Branch, Alberta: Alberta Forest Service Collection.

From 1880s-1940s, mines on Christie Mine Ridge (Map 2), left of photo, supplied coal to Pincher Creek. Over the years, some mines were Richard Murtland Sr's 'Victory', Theodore Neumann's 'Meridian', Scott & MacLane's 'Crescent', Tom Sparrow's 'Beauvais', and W.R & Bishop Wilson's mine. This is view south from Jim Mitchell's homestead NE13-5-2-5. (Back left) Victoria Peak (Map 5). (Mid-centre) Brooke's Coulee. In this 1942 photo, we see the ranch of Ernie & Eleanora Gietz. Daughter, Beverley, is a retired Chief Justice of the Supreme Court. The road into the ranch came from the left background, along the edge of the hill, across the Great Northern Railway coal mine lease.

1932, Jim Mitchell Sr. cabin to east of Mill Creek and west of Christie mine. (L to R) Back row: Peg Mitchell and Jim Mitchell, Sr. Front: Charlie Mitchell holding Jim, Jr. Viewing north, at the bottom of the steep ridge on the right, was the Link Mine on east bank of Mill Creek. (Map 2) From 1936-1940, Jim, Sr. was pit boss at the Christie mine. Bishop Wilson was manager; Charlie was a fireman and miner while Peg cooked for the miners. Bill Crook, Gus Gamache & Walter Cridland, teamsters, hauled coal to Pincher Creek. Bill Tourond had been a teamster about 1920. Albert Therriault was a miner in late 1920s. My grandfather, George Tyson, hauled Christie coal to his farm in Utopia district but he bought better-quality (harder) lump coal from a Lethbridge mine. Christie mine flooded and was closed in the early 1940's.

Alice Willock married Cliff Lang in 1930. Cliff grew up on the Robert & Bessie Lang ranch east of Beaver Mines. The Lang family came west to join friends Jack Ledingham and John Skene. All these families were long-time members of Mountain Mill Church.

Wilbur and Cliff Lang were great friends of my father, Ralph. With other Beaver Mines men Cliff mined at Butte, MT, about 1930. He was then a miner at Christie mine with Wilbrod Clavel, John Mikilak, Vic Sulava and Harry Smith. Cliff worked in the oil boom at Turner Valley from 1936-1943.

This is Steve Lynch, Sr.'s, cabin (built after 1925) on the site of Jack and son, Rolla, Good's mine, West ½ -14-5-1-5, just east of the Christie mine. Bert Owens married Vella Good and linked another Good mine underground to the Christie mine (Map 2).

1947, Beauvais School students on retired Christie mine horse. (L to R) Robert Bertram, Ivan McIntee, Charles Murray, Louis Louchart, Doug Primeau, Joyne Bertram, Larry Lang, Leroy Lang. (Right) Albert Therriault farm where many teachers boarded. Beauvais School got its coal from the Link, Mill Creek (McKinnon), Victory and Christie mines.

About 1916 on their homestead, (L to R) Elmo, Wray (father), Wayne, Velda, Pauline (mother) and Vernon Smith on SE6-3-29-4. Jack Smith wasn't born. Once each fall, Wray Smith, hauled coal home from the Christie mine, paying $3.00 per ton. Pauline said the Christie mine was the 'best mine' for coal.

1974, Wayne Smith at Spread Eagle School. (Background) Spread Eagle Mtn. Mrs. Annie Braun hauled coal with her half-starved team from the Christie mine to the school.

Retired Christie mine horses, such as 'Merry Legs', often became school ponies. Kay Leigh recalled her small son, Mel, rode 'Merry Legs' to Cyr School. So Mel could open gates, 'Merry Legs' would put her head down, Mel would slide off over her ears, open the gate and lead her through. To re-mount, horse and boy reversed the process.

In Beaver Mines, 1913, (L to R) Fred & Ann Harley Link with Charlie, Bert, Dave and Myrtle. Fred and brother, Bert, bought a coal lease from McLaren Lumber in about 1905. They opened the Link Coal Co mine on the east bank of Mill Creek, Sec 25-5-2-5. Nearby was A.D. McKinnon's 'Mill Creek' mine, on the west bank of Mill Creek, on Sec 36-5-2-5. From 1907-1915, Albert mined the Link mine alone. He sold the lease to William Hamilton from Passburg. (Map 2). When I was a child, people would go to similar private mines for their winter supply of coal.

In about 1907, Wenzel and Louise Cisar, with Jim. They homesteaded in Gladstone Valley Sec 9-5-2-4. Wenzel was a miner who worked in the Link and other local mines. Frank recalled his dad, Wenzel, found horse skeletons in a mine with their hides preserved. In an explosion, Wenzel was badly burned, but after a long convalescence, he reovered.

(Right) The black stripe in this 2010 photo is the coal vein visible at McLaren's Point (near the skyline) on the road from Mountain Mill to Gladstone Valley. This vein ran through the Link and Mill Creek mines.

The arrow points to the trail that in 2010 dropped eastward into Mill Creek from the Gladstone Valley road. My Vroom family followed this trail past the old Link mine (Map 2) to ride from our ranch at Beaver Mines to Beauvais Lake and Twin Butte.

About 1960, (L-R) Stanley Babin, Antoinette Babin (George) Biron, Mary Babin Bucar, and John Babin. In 1897, George Biron staked a coal claim on NE33-5-2-5, Canyon Creek Ranch. (Map 2).

In 1928, two bulls fighting in front of the remains of the tunnel entrance to Western Coal & Coke Co. mine at the south end of the village of Beaver Mines. This was the first homestead of George Ballantyne, on SW10-6-2-5 (Map 2).

These two McClelland family photos are at the site of the West Canadian Collieries Adanac Mine No. 2, established in 1947. The site is near Byron Creek on Sec 25-6-4-5.

These are the remains of the Adanac mine building in 2018. The owner, West Canadian Collieries, was a French-based company which founded the coal mine at Bellevue in 1905. Mines were dangerous. The father of my Aunt Margaret (Alfred) Vroom was killed in the 1914 Hillcrest mine disaster.

1881, view upstream of the Kootenai River before it was flooded for the Waterton Dam. This is typical of where coal mines such as John Smith & Jim Fitzpaatrick (Sec 35-4-28-4) and William Smith (Sec 26-4-28-4) operated (Map 2). The work of Dominion Surveyor, George Dawson, initiated much of the early development of SW Alberta coal mines. Credit: Library and Archives Canada / PA-168943

1912, Peter Christensen homestead SE16-4-28-4, south side of Drywood Creek and west of Kootenai River. This was to south of Daniel Fitzpatrick mine (SE3-5-28-4) and Jim Gilruth mine (N½ 27-4-28-4 1914-1934) which were north of Drywood Creek.

About 1911, Emil and Annie Jack on the west side of their home in the Robert Kerr district. The Jack family got coal out of the canyon on Chipman (Indianfarm) Creek (Map 2) to heat their home and use for cooking. One mine on Chipman Creek was on Sec 34-5-29-4. It was operated by Thomas Nash 1902 to 1913. Toots Hochstein recalled there was a tunnel dug into the hill. It wasn't good coal.

This view is SW up Chipman Creek Canyon which was the site 1914-1915 of Billy McFarlane & Lewis Stuckey coal mine on Sec 27-5-29-4 (Map 2). This was SW of the Ben Harder place, the old NWMP Indian Farm. Dave Harder recalled finding buffalo bones in this canyon.

This 2015 photo shows the remnants of Marlow's mine (right mid-foreground) on SW1-8-1-5, NE of Lundbreck. From 1924-1927 the mine was operated by Ed Marlow and Walter Gardner. From 1934-1937 it was known as the Quick Flame mine and was operated by Gardner and the Rhodes Bros. (Harold, William, and Philip). Roy Bent, who worked in the mine, recalled that a sudden spring rain flooded the coulee in which the mine was located. The flood swept the mine shack away, really scaring Roy.

About 1910, Walter and Jennie Rowe Gardner on their ranch in T10-R3-W5 in the Maycroft district. Walter was a geologist who discovered many coal mines in the Lundbreck area. In about 1912, Walter and Jennie moved to his place on Kootenay Lake at 'Gardner's Landing' where Jennie's younger sisters, Ethel and Gladys joined them. The Gardners travelled regularly to the Lundbreck area until the death of Jennie and their young daughter, Margaret, in 1923.

About 1920, (L to R) Jack Morden, George Riviere as young men. (Left) Turtle Mtn and Frank Slide; (Middle) Crowsnest Mtn. Jack and the Riviere brothers brought huskies from the Yukon, which they used as sled dogs in winter and pack dogs in summer. To protect their paws, the dogs wore buckskin moccasins when there was no snow. Jack was one of many who searched for the fabled Lost Lemon mine.

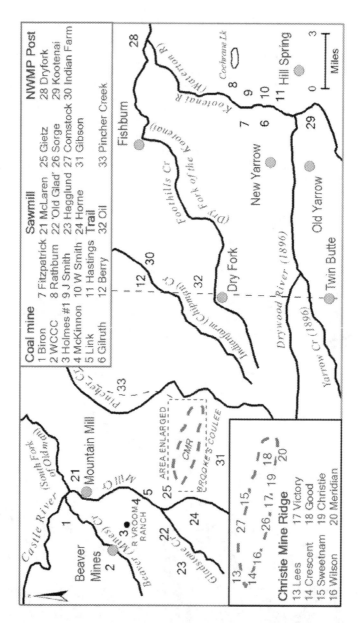

**MAP 2  COAL MINES and SAWMILLS, Beaver Mines to Yarrow, 1875-1945**
**Coal mine**: Berry, Biron, Christie, Crescent, Fitzpatrick, Gilruth, Good**Error! Bookmark not defined.**, Hastings, Holmes #1, Lees, Link, McKinnon ('Mill Creek' mine), Meridian, Rathburn, J Smith, W Smith, Sweetnam, Victory, Western Coal & Coke Co, Wilson  **Sawmill**: Comstock, Gietz, William 'Old Glad' Gladstone, Hagglund, Horne, McLaren, Sorge  **NWMP Post**: Dry Fork, Indian Farm, Kootenai   **Other:** Brooke's Coulee, Christie Mine Ridge.

**MAP 2** (continued): **Post Office:** Beaver Mines, Dry Fork, Fishburn, Hill Spring, Mountain Mill, New Yarrow, Old Yarrow, Twin Butte **Creek, River:** Beaver (Mines), Carbondale (Railway), Castle (South Fork of the Oldman), Dry Fork of the Kootenai (Foothills), Gladstone, Indianfarm (Chipman), Mill, Pincher, Waterton (Kootenai), Yarrow (North Fork of the Kootenai River) **Lake:** Cochrane (Strawberry)

From 1890, there were many coal mines near Lundbreck. Mners included Matt Holloway, James Galbraith's 'Tomato Kid' and John 'Peg Leg' Morris' 'Black Diamond' mine. Viewing south, a light snow in the Fall 2015 faintly marks the trail (mid-photo) along which a narrrow gauge railway ran near Lundbreck (located to upper right of photo). Horses had a difficult time pulling the little mine cars from the mine in the Crowsnest River bottom to the mill above, located between Hwy. 3 and the river valley.

This is the derelict Holmes #1 coal mine operated by Frank Holmes when I was a child (Map 2). It was about 1 mile south of Beaver Mines on the road to Gladstone Valley which ran past our ranch. This shows how small miners made a living selling coal to the locals, who brought their own teams to haul the coal away.

About 1940, (L to R) Elsie holding Louie and Annie with Lady on the Smith Ranch SE30-2-1-5. Elsie recalls that by 1942 the Link coal mine (Map 2) on the east bank of Mill Creek**Error! Bookmark not defined.** was just a hole. She and Annie would throw a rope into the hole, slide down the rope into the mine, put coal in gunny sacks, climb back up the rope, haul the sacks out of the mine and take the coal home on their horses. Their father, Harry, was a miner in the Christie mine for short time but disliked the work.

Dad liked to add fun to almost any occasion. For the 1936 Castle River Stampede parade, he dressed my 7-year-old brother, Bill, as a prospector. Dad made 'hair and whiskers' from a sheep pelt. Bill rode Smokey and led Baby Darling, two goats that I trained to ride. Dad put a small pack on Baby Darling and tied it with a real 'diamond hitch', a special knot used to keep a load securely fastened atop a pack animal.

1940 Pincher Creek Fair and Rodeo parade. (L) Wilbrod Clavel, fireman at the Christie Mine (Map 2), leading a mule that worked in the mine. (R) Unknown, leading pony carrying a pack and prospector's gear.

In the western section of the 1954 Waterton Days parade, (L to R) Andy Russell, Rey Marr and Bill Lammers of Twin Butte, himself an old-time prospector, Bill is leading his donkey loaded with gear. There's a Dominion flag tied to the donkey's pack. Credit: John Russell

1954 Waterton Days parade. (L) Harley H. Boswell, manager of the Prince of Wales hotel since the 1930s. (R) Ralph Vroom, wearing his favourite hat, and dressed as he normally would to guide hunting parties into the mountains. Dad's leading one of his many well-trained pack horses.

# *MAKE ME A COWBOY AGAIN*

♫♫ Backward, turn backward, oh time with your wheels,
Airplanes, wagons and automobiles.
Let me ride out on the prairie and stay.
Make me a cowboy again for a day. ♫♫

In Lundbreck, 1926, (L to R) Jack Evans, Bert Connelly, Bill Bennett, Len Tomas, and Doug McWilliams in front of the Windsor Hotel. They're on their way to Winnipeg and the Peter Welsh Stampede. With broncs and working cowboys, Welsh took rodeos to the East.

About 1948, my brother Bill Vroom, worked for Peter's son, Josie, riding jumping horses for Cliff Cross, owner of the Buckhorn Ranch.

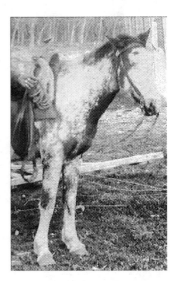

(Left) In 1900, Logie McWhirter rode from Judith Basin, MT, SE of Great Falls, up the Old North Trail, to Pincher Creek. He opened only two gates the entire trip. He rode on a pack saddle as he couldn't afford a regular saddle. He carried his violin.

(Right) Logie rode this cow pony to Pincher Creek.

Sadie Bevan, 15 years in 1909. Joe Bevan, Sr and children Joedy, Sadie, Alice and Dora moved to Park View district in 1907. They settled a mile east of the Nels Ekelund family. Their post office was Waterton Mills. About 1910, Joedy Bevan, along with Kootenai Brown, Klem Pedersen, Choteau Reed, Gus West and Jack Hazzard, worked building the road from Pincher to Waterton (now Hwy. 6). In 1912, Joe sold out to Harry Jenkins.

Lyde Christensen attended the Old Yarrow School. Sadie met Lyde at a dance at Bill & Mamie Thornton's homestead. They married in 1911 and moved to Lyde's homestead SW12-3-29-4, later part of the Shoderee ranch.

Fred Neville was one of thousands of young men in Europe who dreamed of becoming a cowboy in the 'Wild West' of Canada. In 1884, at 14 years, he left England, enlisting with the NWMP at Winnipeg in 1891. Note Fred's pipe, gun and leather pants.

Fred was one of many men who resigned from the NWMP, proved up on homesteads and became ranchers. While at Fort Whoop-Up, Fred met Alice Webster, daughter of pioneer Samuel Webster. In 1894 Fred and Alice married and moved to their homestead SW16-2-28-4, west of Mountain View, AB. In the 1910s, Fred had a grazing lease in this area, to the east of the Belly River.

Fred Pope resigned from the NWMP to prove up SE18-6-1-5 just downstream from Mountain Mill. Here about 1945 are the Pope daughters (L to R) Louisa 'Weasie' (William) Lynch, Nelly (Luverne) Clemens, Agnes Emily (Bob) Stillman, Elizabeth (Ed) Gamache, Mary Ann (Alex) Gervais, Louise 'Lucy' (Gordon) Remington. Not shown is Victoria (George) Fenton. The Stillmans were my Vroom family's neighbours to the west. I often visited Mrs. Stillman as I rode to and from Gladstone Valley School. I sometimes visited Mrs. Gamache and Mrs. Lynch while looking for stray horses.

(Above left) 1912, Frenchy Riviere with son Henri wearing angora chaps. In 1897, Frenchy was a packer for the Klondike Gold Rush. About 1901, he returned to breaking horses at the Locky Bell Ranch, west of Pincher Creek. (Above right) 1906, Charlie Mitchell travelling by covered wagon with his parents, Wash & Belle from Boise, ID to Mountain Mill, AB. In 1926, my Dad bought Charlie's ranch, south of Beaver Mines.

About 1920, Jim Chisholm on his ranch north of Mountain View performing trick roping on 'Sailor'. Jim came from Ontario in 1898 to homestead SE30-2-27-4. He worked out for the Cochrane and Richard Wellman ranches.

Richard Wellman came from the US in 1902 to homestead SW10-2-27-4. In 1934, his son, John, moved to the Park View district and bought the Waterton dairy from Doug Oland.

About 1943, (L to R) Philip Big Swan and Pete LaGrandeur at Peigan Siding, east of Brocket. Pete was stockman for Indian Affairs on the Reserve. Pete's brother, Ed, had been Farm Instructor for the Reserve from 1914-1919. In 1924, Pete won the Canadian Bucking Horse Championship and the Canadian All Around at the Calgary Stampede. Big Swan, also a skilled cowboy, was Hereditary Chief of the Peigan (Piikani Nation).

Part of the historic 1908 roundup of buffalo getting close to the corrals in Ravalli, MT. After chases like this 40 mile run, fine horses could never be ridden again. The terrible strain foundered, exhausted or killed them. 716 head of Pablo-Allard buffalo were shipped to Alberta, and formed the base of the herds at Banff and Waterton Park.

(Above left) Emil Jack on 'Annie', his favourite horse, named for his wife, Annie Hescott. He's on their ranch in the Spread Eagle district. (Above right) About 1905, Ted Hardy dressed in his 'Sunday best' with his handsome saddle horse. Ted's homestead NW15-4-30-4 was just west of my father-in-law George Annand's homestead SE14-4-30-4. Ted was a great friend of my uncle Thomas B. Tyson.

Although Washington and Belle Mitchell were in their 50s, in 1906 they travelled by covered wagon from Idaho to homestead NE16-5-2-5 in Gladstone Valley. Here in about 1920, 'Wash' was a talented horse trader and raconteur of yarns. Wash and the John and Harry Truitt families were early homesteaders in 'the Valley'. I'm related to the Truitt and Mitchell families through my aunt Ruby Mitchell (Harold) Vroom.

Horse packers were an integral part of cowboy life. Here in 1913, the Alberta-BC Boundary Survey crew is at Kelly's Camp on the Castle River. The packer at right may be Jimmy Burgess Miller, Sr, who was the Castle River forest ranger stationed at Kelly's Camp from about 1912-1918. Jimmy was a friend of Ralph Vroom and Sam Hassett.

Vern Albiston grew up near Taylorville, SE of Cardston. In 1928, across from Lake Linnet, Waterton, Vern is a guide for Morris Bros. Guides & Outfitters, run by Malvina Morris. He later worked for George Riviere as a guide/wrangler/packer. In 1965, Vern followed Delance Strate and Norm Hicklin as Park maintenance foreman.

About 1924, Vern's wife, Martha, came to Waterton with her father, Billy McEwen, who by then was a widower. They lived near Geo and Betsy Annand, with Billy's uncle, Jack Gladstone and his wife, the widow Marie Rose Gervais Tourond.

Arnold Davidson and Hazel Findlay married in 1912. Arnold was the son of Mountain View homesteader Olof Davidson. About 1902, when he was 10 years old, Arnold was a night herder on the historic Cochrane Ranch.

In 1884, as a result of several bitterly cold winters near Calgary, the British American Ranche Co. took a lease between the Waterton and Belly Rivers known as the Cochrane Ranch. It was sold in 1904 and renamed the Church Ranch (LDS).

Arnold and Hazel's daughter, Vella, married Pat Carnell, Jr., of Waterton. Pat was the son of Park View homesteaders, Pat, Sr. and Hannah McGlennning Carnell. In 1914, my mother, Mollie, her parents and brother, Tom, immigrated from Ambleside, Eng, to work for Hannah's uncle Hector McGlenning, in the Fishburn district SE of Pincher Creek.

View west to the 'table' part of Table Mtn and Beaver Mines Lk below it (Map 5). In 1910 my Dad, Ralph Vroom, and some friends had a horse race on the 'table'. In the 1930s and 1940s, Table Mtn was a popular day ride for guests of the Buckhorn Ranch in Gladstone Valley.

In 1950, my brother, Bill Vroom, was a 19-years old wrangler for the Buckhorn Ranch where he worked from 1948-1951. He was a horse packer for the Dept. of Mines and Technical Surveys supporting topographical survey crews in 1952, the Mayo-Old Crow map and, in 1953, the MacMillan River map near the confluence of the Yukon and Teslin Rivers. In 1954 Bill became head saddle maker at Kenway Saddle & Leather, Calgary. He joined the Banff warden service in 1955 and was stationed in the Eisenhower, Lake Louise, Clearwater, Bryant Creek, Mistaya, Spray River and Healy Creek districts. Bill was a grizzly bear expert and a 1960s pioneer in the development of mountain rescue techniques using cables and helicopter slings.

In 1948, Dave Truitt on 'Custer' at the JO Ranch, Gladstone Valley, the homestead of Philip and Elizabeth Klauzinski NE17-5-2-5. Dave was the son of Harry & Bessie Mitchell Truitt.

Cowboys became packers for survey crews. Here in 1953, Bill Vroom, head packer stands out-of-sight encouraging the lead horse to get the other packhorses safely across the Yukon River. They were with Canada Dept. of Mines, topographical survey crew.

Summer 1953, Dave Harder, packer for Canada Dept. of Technical Surveys, at the pinnacle of Font Mtn., southwest of Pincher Creek.

1954, Dave Harder, head packer, Dept. of Technical Surveys, with packtrain crossing the Bull River at Sulphur Creek, north of Fernie, BC. They were surveying for the 'Fernie 82G' topo map.

1953, Dave Harder on Drywood Mtn. Looking west, mid-backgournd, Castle Mtn. (left) and Castle Turret (mid-right), Victoria Peak (far right). As horse packer, Dave climbed 49 peaks in SW AB with 'Tech Surveys' in the summers of 1953-1954.

This 1963 view from Vimy Ridge, Waterton Park, is of the grasslands leased in 1882 by rancher W.A. Henry. There is no history of this pioneer whose grazing lease included the lands around Middle and Lower Kootenai Lakes.

Ranchers became Park wardens. Taken across from Lake Linnet, (L to R) Wallace Gladstone and Alf Clark are wearing angora chaps. They were Waterton wardens the summers of 1919-1920.

Grazing leases existed in Waterton into the 1940s. About 1930, an unknown cowgirl herds cattle on Pass Creek Flats. Viewing north, this was Kootenai Brown's 'Pass Creek' homestead on SE31-1-29-4 where he lived with Nichemoos and stableman, Charles Spence, from about 1892 to 1905. About 1876, Kootenai Brown and Fred Kanouse ran a mile long horse race on these flats against the Kootenai Indians.

1935, (Standing) Frank Carpenter; (seated L to R) James and Charlie Riviere, Jerry Spence, guides for Riviere Horse Rentals, Red Rock Canyon, Waterton. In August, their pack and saddle horses were conscripted to pack supplies to fight the Boundary Fire on Upper Waterton Lake.

1940, Etta Platt on my beloved White Wings at our family horse rentals, Red Rock Canyon. One of the few times Dad cried was when he told us that White Wings had starved to death when trapped in crystallized snow out on the winter range.

(Left) 1940, Bessie Vroom, on Queen Mab, Red Rock Canyon. My mom, Mollie, brother Don, and I were renting out our horses for much-needed income. Dad was Overseas.

(Above right) Years later, as a teacher in Waterton in 1947, I was very surprised to receive this sterling silver brooch of a horse and saddle with Spanish-style tapaderos. It was from a US airman who'd rented a horse from us in 1940. By serendipity, the brooch was delivered from the US in a package addressed simply as: "To Bessie Vroom, who used to live at Red Rock Canyon, Waterton Park, Alberta".

(Above left) About 1925, two cowgirls (L to R) Edith 'Toots' Jack amd Velda Smith. (Above right) About 1943, (Right) Dorothy 'Dixie' Holroyd and cousin, Connie, at Cedar Cabin, Waterton. (Background) Vimy Ridge. Dix's father, Bo, was Chief Warden.

(Above) In Waterton, 1940, Etta Platt is wearing chaps she designed and embroidered using coloured wool. She is holding Toy, owned by Betty Giddie, daughter of warden Jack Giddie. Vella Baptiste (Jolliffe) wore an embroidered vest and skirt made by Etta in the 1912 Calgary Stampede parade. The set is in the collection of Glenbow Archives, Calgary. Etta sent my Dad, Ralph, many of her photos when he was Overseas in WW2.

(Above right) 1939, Margaret Hoschka rode in the 1938 Calgary Stampede parade. In 1942, she married Charlie Riviere. Margerie Shenton recalled that, as part of their family's food, Margaret canned elk meat in stoneware.

# SWEETHEART OF THE ROCKIES

The charming waltz, When It's Springtime in the Rockies, is from the 1943 film 'Silver Spurs' starring Roy Rogers. The song expresses the happy anticipation of a cowboy returning to his 'sweetheart of the Rockies'. The waltz was very popular at dances in Pincher Creek and district. Photos of sweethearts at weddings and anniversaries remain treasured memories for families.

Hazel Truitt married Bob Tourond in November 1938. My dad and I attended their wedding dance at the 'old' Gladstone Valley School (far left) on SE22-5-2-5, under Table Mtn. Hazel was very well-liked and was going to be sadly missed by everyone in 'the Valley'. I vividly remember, during the midnight lunch break, the crowd stood up and joined hands. We formed a circle around Bob and Hazel and sang the haunting song 'The Red River Valley'. When we sang, 'we will miss your bright eyes and sweet smile', there wasn't a dry eye in the place. We ended with, 'Just remember Gladstone Valley and the people who loved you so true', and were left with a real sense of loss.

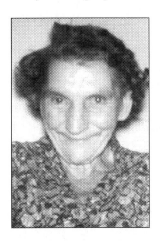

Bob Tourond was the great-grandson of 'Old Glad' Gladstone. His mother, Helen Bowes, (far left in 1962) was the daughter of Harriet Gladstone and a half-sister of Sen. James Gladstone. In 1915 she married Bill Tourond (right), the son of Vic and Lena Marie Gervais Tourond, Mountain Mill. Bill hauled ice to the King Edward Hotel in Pincher.

Harry Truitt and Bessie Mitchell on their wedding day in Boise, ID, 1899. In 1905, Harry and George Smith travelled by covered wagon to Gladstone Valley. In 1906, Bessie and her parents, Wash and Belle Mitchell, followed by covered wagon. Wash homesteaded NE16-5-2-5. Harry homesteaded SE22-5-2-5. George Smith built the Buckhorn Ranch (Map 5) on NE18-5-2-5. Bessie's sister, Ruby, married my uncle Harold Vroom.

In 1895, John Truitt, Harry's brother, married Melcina "Cinie" Newton. In 1906, they travelled with their 6 children by train from Illinois to their homestead NE22-5-2-5 at the entrance to Pleasant Valley. Their large log home faced a magnificent view across Gladstone Valley to Victoria Peak. For extra income, John frieighted by team and wagon from Pincher Creek to the ranch of Timothe Lebel in Gladstone Valley. All the Truitt sons played the violin beautifully.

(Left) In 1896, Jane Rae married William Barclay, Sr. in Scotland. In 1905, they homesteaded Sec 9-5-2-5 in Gladstone Valley, clearing dense bush and tress. Before 1912, their children rode 5 miles to attend the Archie Vroom School on NW35-5-2-5. Their post office was Mountain Mill. For many years, William was Secretary-Treasurer of Gladstone Valley School.

Here in 1907, the 1st (Old) St. Martin's Church on SW6-9-1-5, Livingstone district. This Anglican Church is now in Heritage Park, Calgary, but cemetery markers remain noting the names of oldtimers buried. The 2nd (New) St. Martin's was on NE2-10-2-5, Maycroft district. It was closed in 1998 and moved to Brocket as St. Cyprian's Anglican.

(L to R) About 1920, Agnes Hewitt, Ed Hewitt (siblings), Bob Hewitt (groom), and Selina Ward (bride) on their wedding day at Jack Hewitt's ranch on NW14-9-1-5 in the Porcupine Hills. Selina made and decorated her cake, a skill she learned in England. The Hewitts were members of St. Martin's Anglican Church, Livingstone district.

In 1947 (L to R) Edith Hewitt (bridesmaid in blue) Jack Peterson (groom), Robina Hewitt (bride), Bessie Vroom, (maid-of-honour in pink) at the home of Bob and Selina Hewitt, Pincher Creek. Doug Hewitt was Best Man. The wedding was in St. John's Anglican. Emma Tustian played the music. Jack and Robina's ceremony was the same as that of Princess Elizabeth and Prince Phillip held the previous day! Robina is my lifelong best friend. In the early 1940s I spent a lot of happy times with the Hewitt family on their ranch 'up the North Fork'.

(Above left) In 1936 Rose Chiesa and Primo Lant were married by Father O'Dea in St. Anthony's Roman Catholic Church, Beaver Mines. Her parents, Angelo and Ossana Chiesa raised 8 children on their place on Screwdriver Creek which was the homestead of Melvin Cain. (Above right) St. Anthony's in 2011. There are references to St Anthony's Mission in Beaver Mines (Map 3) as early as 1913. Several daughters of George & Toni Biron were married in St. Anthony's.

Built in 1904, Trinity Lutheran Church stood 10 km south of Pincher Creek on Hwy 6. Previously, services were held in the Crook School. Also known as the 'Cridland' Parish, the church (here in about 1940) burned in 1949 but the cemetery still stands in 2020.

In 1898, Bertha Bradtke (far left) married Frank Crook. Frank sang in the Boys Choir at Salisbury Cathedral, Eng He came to work at a sawmill near Cowley and met Bertha at Mountain Mill where she and her mother were cooking for a crew of McLaren sawmill men. Frank homesteaded NE30-5-29-4 in the Crook district where Lutheran families included Bastian, Braatz, Bradtke, Geberdt, Hahn, Hammer, Neumann, Schoening, Schultz, Sorge and Wittkopf.

St. Henry's Catholic Church, Yarrow district, was built in 1906 on land donated by Frank Speth from his homestead SE24-4-29-4.

(Above right) In 1902, Gus Hochstein married Mary Schulte in Nebraska. Their homestead NE26-4-29-4 was in the Robert Kerr district. They were a founding family of St. Henry's Church. Mary was a talented seamstress. Some of her sewn garments are artifacts held at Kootenai Brown Pioneer Village in Pincher Creek.

(Above left) On July 15, 1929, Alice Riviere married Alphie Primeau in St. Henry's Church. 50 guests attended the wedding breakfast at her parents' (Map 5) Victoria Peak Ranch on SW 21-4 -1-5 (above right about 1930), the home of Frenchy and Nellie Riviere. The Primeau's son, Jimmy, was a friend of mine. In the summer of 1935, I stayed with the Primeaus while Mom was down east getting treatment for her arthritis.

On January 4, 1921, my parents Ralph Vroom & Mollie Tyson were married by Rev. J. Newton Wilkinson in the manse of the Presbyterian Church, Pincher Creek. The manse, to the left of the Church, was built in 1898. Used with the kind permission of the Pincher Creek and District Historical Society Accession No. 976.14.01

In July 1910, Ethel Duthie married Frank McLaughlin at her parent's home in Pincher Creek. They honeymooned in a tent on Knight's Lake, Waterton. In operation at the time was Lee's Tented Village (shown here) on Middle Waterton Lake. At the far left is the Bill Aldridge family cabin where Bill and Annie lived in the winters with 13 children until 1904. In the summers, they lived at Oil City where Bill was the first in Alberta to commercialize oil.

Lalia and Jack Bechtel married in Pincher Creek in 1917. Their home quarter was SW35-29-3-4 in the Spread Eagle district. Here in 1942, they are celebrating their 25th anniversary at the 'Forks' Cabin, Red Rock Canyon, Waterton. They had spent their honeymoon at this cabin. When built, it was known as the 'Hidden' or 'Lost' Cabin. In 1918, a map called the cabin a 'stopover or cache". In the 1920s, it was home to warden 'Bo' Holroyd and wife, Constance. The Forks Cabin stood until about 1949.

In 1921, Mollie Vroom on their honeymoon in the Castle River Forest Reserve and mountains, southwest of Beaver Mines. Mom, an accomplished rider, is sidesaddle on Jack (middle). On far right, Ralph's dog, Jock, is sitting behind the saddle. As a pup, Dad taught Jock to ride so that he could accompany Dad on long hunting/pack trips.

Carl Carlson and Cecile Ada Joyce at the time of their marriage about 1923. They moved to Waterton in 1925. Like many locals, Carl worked on building the Prince of Wales Hotel. Cecile visited Waterton as a girl with her parents, Ed and Bella, who homesteaded NE12-5-30-4 in the Robert Kerr district. Well-liked oldtimers, the Carlson family is buried in the Waterton cemetery.

In 1954, Oliver Oliver and Arletta Goble celebrate their 50th wedding anniversary in Waterton. Both Bohne and Goble families were part of the Mormon hand-cart pioneers into Utah Territory 1856-1860. Their families later travelled by covered wagon from Utah to west of Aetna, AB. Arletta's family came in 1898. Oliver's family followed in 1900. He worked as a cowboy for several large local ranches. They married in Aetna and brought their six children to Waterton in 1927. The Gobles, along with their sons Frank and Ken, were part of the local social and business fabric for decades. Frank was groomsman when I married Geordie Annand.

From 1911-1913, Chris Christianssen worked in the Henry Hanson sawmill 1½ miles downstream from the Park on the Waterton River, near the Jenkins ranch. Chris and Chrissie McKenzie wed in Lethbridge about 1921. In 1923, Chris joined the Parks service. They raised therir three childrn in Waterton. In 1956, Chris retired as a Park warden. For many years, his sons, Jack and Ed, were Park wardens in Waterton and Kootenay National Parks, respectively. They were life-long friends of my husband, Geordie Annand. Chrissie was a childhood friend of Betty Annand Baker from 1914 when the Annand and McKenzie families lived north of Mountain View, near Caldwell, AB.

Wedding of Annie Halton and Walter Moser, Pincher Creek United Church, 1929. Standing (L to R): Jim Halton, Matt Halton, David Halton (boy), Walter Moser (groom), Annie Halton (bride), Seth Halton (boy), Harry Halton (bride's father), Sam Halton. Seated (L to R): Joan Halton, Dorothy Halton, Mary Alice Halton (bride's mother), Ernie Halton, Joe Thornley (brother of Mary Alice).

John Bond and Elizabeth Creighton wed in North Dakota, 1901. They raised seven children on their Hillsboro district homestead NE36-7-29-4. Their daughter Alvina came as a child from ND. She married Wilbrod Clavel of the Beauvais district. Marcus Bond married Ida Martin, and Phyllis Bond married Cy Truitt, all of Gladstone Valley. Violet 'Vi' Bond, who loved to fish, married Milford O'Bray. Vi lived in Waterton for many years. The Bonds were great friends of my Vroom family.

Bride Hannah McGlenning, Fishburn district, stands behind her husband Pat Carnell, Sr. who homesteaded on the Dry Fork, NW12-5-29-4. Hannah travelled west with her parents from Meaford, ON, in 1897. They were married by Presbyterian minister Rev. Hugh Grant in 1898. My grandparents George and Mary Tyson worked for Hannah's brother, Hector, when they immigrated to Canada in 1914. While working for 'Hec' they learned Canadian farming methods. In 1915, Hannah and Pat moved to the Park View district to run a dairy on their homestead SE30-2-29-4. After Pat's death, Hannah married Jim Presley of Waterton, where she and her family were longtime residents.

Newly married, John Bruns sits with his bride, Trace Bruening, after their wedding in Pincher Creek, 1911. (Standing) Attendants, Fred and Mary Kunkel (Mark) Weiller Bruns. John homesteaded W½-SW10-5-30-4 and Fred on S½ -SE18-4-29-4. Fred's son was Harold. I met Harold and his wife, Gada, when she was matron of the Pincher Creek High School dormitory where I boarded 1941-1942. Harold drove the school bus from Brocket. They were extremely kind to all young people over the years.

Logie McWhirter and Ina Dyer wed in 1905 in Idaho. Logie homesteaded NE6-5-29-4 on the Dry Fork in the Cyr district. Logie was a talented violinist and baseball player. Both he and Ina won trophies from the local shooting club. Their daughter, Essie, married Orville Cox, Jr, the grandson of Bill Aldridge who commercialized the first oil in Alberta at Oil City.

(Left) St. Michael's Roman Catholic Church, Pincher Creek about 1920.

(Above right) Alfred Pelletier wed Philomene LaGrandeur in 1895. Alfred arrived in Pincher in 1888 and was a noted stockman. Philomene's parents, Moise and Julia, settled at LaGrandeur Crossing on the Oldman River in 1882. Her LaGrandeur siblings were great friends of my parents. Emery and Pete were Canadian and World Champion Bronc Riders. Emma married Walter Cridland, an oldtime teamster. Albert married Lizzie Klauzinski, daughter of Philip (NE17-5- 2-5), Gladstone Valley.

When homesteaders settled the Canadian West, many natural features were unnamed. Some of the settlers named geographical features for their sweethearts.

In 1923, my mother Mollie remained in Beaver Mines while my dad Ralph was logging at Paulson in the West Kootenay region of BC My dad named nearby Mollie Creek for my mother. Mollie Creek (49°09'43"N, 118°08'45"W) flows southwest into Josh Creek, west into McRae Creek, and finally into Christina Lake.

(Far left) John Niblock, CPR Superintendent, Mountain Division, 1887-1910, named Claresholm for his wife, Clare (here in 1903). Credit P. Niblock

(Left) My Uncle Harold Vroom homesteaded SE32-5-2-5. In 1910, he married Ruby Mitchell. Uncle Harold named Ruby Creek (Map 3), a tributary of Beaver (Mines) Creek, for his sweetheart and new wife.

## MAP 3  BEAVER MINES and MOUNTAIN MILL DISTRICTS, circa 1935:
**Landmark, river, lake:** the 'Big' and 'Little' Hills on our ranch, the roads to Grandpa Oscar Vroom and Gladstone Valley, Beaver (Mines) Creek, Beaver Mines and the Roundhouse, Burmis and CPR line, Castle (South Fork) River, Castle River Stampede Grounds, Gilmore Ridge, Lee Lake, Mill Creek, Mountain Mill, Ruby Creek, Screwdriver Creek, and the shortcut to Coalfields School. **Ranch/residence:** John Babin, Stanley Babin, George & Sarah Ballantyne, George & Antoinette Babin Biron, Bill Bremner, Maj. Edward 'Ted' & Mabel Bruce, John & Mary Babin Bucar, George Crosbie, Bill & Isabel Eddy, Jack Eddy, Edward & Elizabeth Pope Gamache, Gus Gamache, Gordon and his mother Jessie Wilgar Hamilton, Earl & Margaret Fitzpatrick Hollinbeck, Louise Riley (Frank) Holmes, Gillis Currie, Edward & Elsie Crosbie Joyce, Jack Joyce, John Kobza, Fred & Ann Harley Link, George Lowery, Ken and Ina McDowall, 'W.D.' & Emma Price McDowall, Joe & Maria Motil, John & Veroni Kulkosky Oczkowski, Mike & Verona Pirozak, Horace & Elizabeth Sicotte, Spellman Bros., Bob & Agnes Pope Stillman, Harold & Ruby Mitchell Vroom, Lewis & Grace Currie Warren, Andrew & Steffina Wojtyla, Harry & Pearl Zurowski.

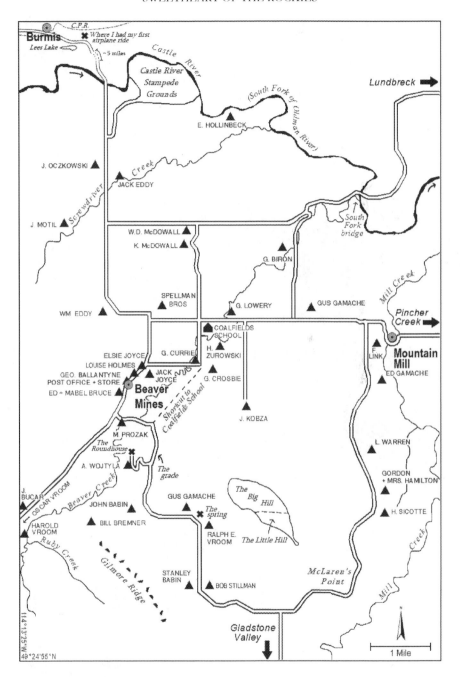

**MAP 3   BEAVER MINES and MOUNTAIN MILL DISTRICTS, circa 1935**

In 1906, Margaret McGlynn married Fred Robbins in Pincher Creek. Their son, Gerald, married my cousin Adeline Cyr. Fred operated the Pincher City livery barn until the 1930s when the Alexandra Hotel burned. He famously said, 'To be an old-timer, you had to be here before the railway', that is, before 1898.

Dora McKarrall and 'JJ' McFarland wed in 1914. JJ bought land from my Uncle Tom 'T.B.' Tyson near Fishburn. Dora taught at Fishburn School 1914 and Utopia School 1920-21. Utopia was built on NE33-4-28-4, land donated by 'Old Jim' Gilruth, uncle to JJ. In about 1883, 'Old Jim' walked north past Chief Moutain to settle near the Kootenai River.

1912, Ambush Woman (Issyo'maki) and husband, Tom Three Persons of the Blood (Kainai) Reserve, Cardston. He's wearing his World Champion Bronc Riding medal won at the 1912 Calgary Stampede. He rode the great 'Cyclone' to a stop. Tom was also an acclaimed calf roper, inspiring many Blood cowboys. Tom was a friend of my dad, Ralph Vroom, and George Riviere.

Jim Gladstone and his war bride, Iris, wed about 1918. He was the son of William Gladstone II and Mary Samat Vandal Johnson. Thousands of Canadian servicemen married European women after WW1 and WW2. My Waterton friends who were war brides were Anna Gladstone and Olga Russell.

# PLAYING A COWBOY SONG

♫♫ I ride along with the doggies and sing,
It's a beautiful day in the early spring,
On my faithful horse, I ride along,
Playing a cowboy song. ♫♫

1912, Fred and Anne Link on the verandah of the McLaren ranch house at Mountain Mill. This is typical of old-time ranch houses with one large upstairs room which was used for community dances. Others, such as Remi Beauvais' ranch house, were also social gathering places for local ranch families.

About 1911, (L to R) Eugene McFarland, George Marcellus, Frank McFarland and Walter Marcellus. Photo taken beside the Waterton River near the McFarland place on SE22-4-28-4. In the 1910s, George played violin with the Col. James Ward orchestra in the Fishburn district. In the 1920s-1930s, he played with the (Mrs.Lola) Altermatt Dance Orchestra. George was decorated for his participation at the Somme in WWI.

About 1930, Charlie 'Chink' Riviere playing fiddle. Charlie grew up on his parents Victoria Peak Ranch (Map 5). It was NW of the Spread Eagle Stampede grounds where Charlie played for open air dances. In 1955, Charlie and my dad Ralph Vroom drove a stagecoach from Fort Macloed to the Calgary Stampede as part of Alberta 50th Jubilee celebrations.

In 1939, (L to R) Etta Brown Platt of Waterton and a niece are playing guitars and singing in harmony. They are set to go to the 1939 Calgary Stampede. Etta was a long-time friend of my parents. From 1933 to 1952, Etta attended Waterton community functions, entertaining the crowd with her singing and sense of humour.

(Left) Violin brought by Logie McWhirter in 1900 when he rode his cow pony from Montana up the Old North Trail to Pincher Creek. The difference between a violin and a fiddle is the type of music that's played. Fiddlers played old-time Western music, as well as step and square dancing, among others.

(Right) The guitar of Charlie Dyson was a prized possession of Bob Thomas. Charlie, an African-American, moved to the SW Alberta before 1890. He was Pincher Creek's first blacksmith. He and his wife, Eliza, settled in the Robert Kerr district. They were highly respected by neighbours including the families of Reg Bird, John Halverson, Henry Pearson, and Nels and Peter Vance.

(Left) Ted 'Dinks' Duffield in 1943. He played the saw with a violin bow. Ted bent the saw to make different notes.

Kay Leigh sitting at her 125 years-old piano in 2004. By 1935, she and brother, Ken McRae (violin), were playing for dances in Twin Butte. During WW2, soldiers came from Fort Macleod to Pincher Creek to dance to Kay and Ken's music.

In the late 1930s, Framac Hall is above the McRobert's Dept Store on the second floor of the brick building on the right.

(Right) On December 31, 1943, I'm wearing my first evening gown to the New Year's Eve Fireman's Ball at Framac Hall where the Ernie Cridland Orchestra (the Radions) played. Friends who attended similar dances included Helen Burns, Walter Cleland, Rita & Vera Cyr, Bob Dennis, Lois Duffield, Otto Gietz, Ernie Haug, Robina Hewitt, Una Hunt, Harry Likuski, Eleanor MacLean, Alex McMurdo, Edith Shenton McRae, Ed Mitchell, Gwen Pearson, 'Bunny' Pelletier, Steve & 'Bugs' Sorge, Shirley Thomas, Lois Topp, Don Vroom.

My gown is a turquoise net princess style dress over a pale green taffeta slip. The pale taffeta showed through the dark turquoise net and made a striking colour for my gown. My mother, Mollie, remodelled another dress and sewed this using a Singer machine that had belonged to her mother, Mary Tyson. In the summer of 1944, I wore this gown to wedding dance of Frank and Audrey Sorge Slapinski, also held in Framac Hall.

(Far left) Tourist Café, Main St, Waterton. Betty Baker sits in a Model T Ford in front of the Beach Café, previously the Palace Dance Hall. In about 1922, her parents, Geo, Sr & Betsy Annand, checked coats and took tickets for jitney dances at "the Palace". My husband, Geordie Annand, recalled that he was about 7 years old. When he got tired, his parens made him a bed on a pile of coats in the corner.

In 1926, the Waterton Dance Pavilion, the largest one in Western Canada. Geordie Annand remembered the heads of large moose, deer, sheep and other wild animals mounted on the pillar. A second floor balcony provided viewing. On the left of the dance floor are two wickets for ticket-taking for jitney dances – a dime apiece or 3 dances for 25 cents. In the mid-1930s, Mart Kenney and his Western Gentlemen famously played here.

In the 1920s & '30s, on Saturday evenings, band and party-goers would ride the *International* to the Glacier NP end of Waterton Lake where Sunday drinking laws and Prohibition didn't apply. The Goat Haunt Chalet, pictured here in about 1930, was the dance hall for revellers. Built in 1924, it was near the site of Henry Hanson's original logging operation of about 1910. From here, Henry moved logs down to his sawmill at Waterton Mills. Logging was done with oxen and horses, which were transported up and the lakes by the steamboat *Gertrude*.

Here at its opening in 1951, the Lions Club Community Hall was the centre for Waterton locals' winter entertainment. In the '50s, Jack Smith (tenor sax), Claude Hammond, Ruth Tench (piano), Doris Robbins (piano and Harry Gresl (accordian) played for New Year's Eve dances which I attended. (Background, left) All Saints Anglican Church, with Prince of Wales Hotel on the hill above.

The Waterton Dischords Orchestra of the '50s and '60s included local residents Stella Schlaht (violin), Eunice Kerr, (piano); Meredith Going (drums), his daughter, Merna (accordion), John Haslam (guitar), Orene Strate (drums). This is John with his wife, Jean, in the backgournd. John was Chief Engineer for the Prince of Wales Hotel after Doug Allison. John and Jean were my life-long friends.

'Mac' McAllister, Pass Creek district warden in Waterton, 1933. Mac was a one-man band, playing for Twin Butte. He pumped the bass drum with one foot, corded dances on the piano and played the harmonica.

Women were square dance callers, along with men. Pam Pittaway (right) was a caller for the Waterton-Lakes E-Dos Square Dance Club in the 1950s and '60s, along with Eunice Kerr and Eileen MacLeod. The Pincher Creek Old Time Dance Club would attend at the Waterton Community Hall.

Tennessee Ernie Ford was famous for his sense of humour and modern Western songs. Here in the 1950s, he poses for Bessie Annand as he stands in the lobby of the Prince of Wales Hotel, Waterton.

In 1925, Eda Johnson (Foster) poses with Vimy Ridge. To the right, in about 1908, Henry Hanson tied logs together and built Waterton's first dance floor. It floated on the shallow water at the outlet of the Maskinonge to the river. This was where the Coal Oil Trail from Waterton to Fort Macleod had crossed, directly east of Fred Kanouse's 1878 ranch. People came from all over southern Alberta to camp. Frank and Ethel McLaughlin rode from Pincher Creek to honeymoon here in July 1910.

(L to R) Audrey Walters Shakleton, Wilf Carter 'Parade Marshal' and Kate Walters are ready to ride in 1979 Calgary Stampede Parade. Wilf was the first Country and Western singing star born in Canada. The lyrics to Wilf's songs were published in the Western Producer weekly magazine and featured at local dances, fairs and stampedes in the 1950s and '60s. He influenced many aspiring singers who ordered their own guitar with 'teach yourself' playing kits from Eaton's catalogue.

Often an entrie family was musical. Here in 1933, the Bruce family plays beside their home at the south end of of Beaver Mines. (L to R) Michael (harmonica), Edward (mandolin-banjo), Mabel (ukulele), Ronald (mandolin-banjo) and Anthony (ukulele).

In 1933, Geroge Ballantyne drives his daughter Elva in a covered sleigh back to school in Pincher. On the left is the old Beaver Mines Opera House (later Dance Hall then Movie Theatre). My brother Don and I would climb the Movie Theatre's dark, narrow rickety stairs to the projection room and peer down on the empty theatre below. The Kootenay and Alberta Railway Co., taking coal from the Western Coal & Coke Co mine in the village, once ran along the Beaver (Mines) Creek bottom to the right of the photo.

Vera and Ruth Tench, daughers of Cliff, 1929 in Beaver Mines. In the 1940s, the "Polka Dots" band members Ruth (piano), Harry Gresl (accordion) and John Babin (violin) were a mainstay of Saturday night dances at Buckhorn Ranch (Map 5). Ruth married Alex White, who came to the Beaver mines ditrict with the Gresl family. Alex's mother was a Gresl. Cliff Tench bought the ranches of Pete McEwen and Billy 'the Kid' Welsh near Mountain Mill.

The 'New' Yarrow School, east of Twin Butte in 2014, was one of a legion of country schools used for community dances. In 1925, the 'Old' School was moved from SW17-4-28-4 near the Drywood Creek to Fred Klunker's land SW19-4-28-4 to become known as the 'New' school.

(L to R) Jack, Isabelle and Bill Eddy 1930 at the Eddy place north of Beaver Mines, 1930 (Map 3). Isabelle played piano for dances at the Women's Institute Hall. One time George Ballantyne, Bill Eddy and others played 'Pedro' so enthusiastically that the floor vibrated wildly, causing Bill and his chair to fall off the stage.

This photo of my husband George 'Geordie' Annand and I appeared in the Lethbridge Herald, December 28, 1968. The caption noted "the 83rd annual Oldtimers Ball was organized by the Lethbridge and District Pemmican Club. This ball is the oldest, continuous year end Ball in Canada." For decades, oldtimers like Billy McEwen never missed this Ball.

I still treasure the rich-brown velvet dress that I'm wearing. My grandmother, Mary Tyson, brought it from England when she immigrated in 1914. The bodice of the dress is a fitted style with a modified sweetheart neckline. A pleated fold of the luxurious material, with golden brown hand-embroidered French knots, frames the neckline. The long, gored, princess-style skirt is finished with a similar piece of material, which is also adorned with golden brown hand-embroidered French knots. Credit: The Lethbridge Herald.

# HOME ON THE RANGE

♫♫ Home, home on the range
Where the deer and the antelope play.
Where never is heard a discouraging word
And the skies are not cloudy all day. ♫♫

In about 1942, this views west onto NE17-5-2-5. (Background) Table Mtn (Map 5) towers above the JO Ranch barn. (Foreground) The homestead barn of Philip and Elizabeth Klauzinski. Their daughter, Elizabeth, Jr, married Albert LaGrandeur, Sr.

Martin Devine homesteaded SE28-5-2-5, between Gladstone Valley and Beaver (Mines) Creek, about 1912. By then, a lot of remaining homestead land was located deep in the foothills. Martin was a neighbor and great friend of my grandfather Oscar Vroom and his son, Harold (Map 5). Here about 1940, George Hagglund is building an addition to Martin's barn.

Viewing east to Pincher Creek, about 1900, the McLaren ranch house (far right) and ranch buildings at Mountain Mill (Map 3). Many skilled cowboys rode for the McLaren ranch, including Robert Clarkson, Wm Dobbie, the 'Gladstone boys' (Robert, Harry and Jack), Bill Lees, Billy Lynch and Alex MacKinnon. My Uncle Harold Vroom carved the name of his sweetheart (and later wife), Ruby Mitchell, inside the ranch's 'Heart' brand on a log in the barn on the far left. The barn was still standing in 2017.

When I was a child, John Babin was our closest neighbour. This was the homestead log barn built by his parents, John Sr and Gertrude Babin on NE33-5-2-5 about 1915 (Map 3). John Jr looked after his aged mother and was an expert violinist. For dances at Gladstone Valley School, he walked the five miles carrying his precious violin. Sometimes John caught a ride with us but he could walk faster than our team could pull a sleigh or wagon. The Babins had an upright piano. After WWII, John tried to get me to play some music while he accompanied me on his violin, but that didn't work out very well. I was all fingers, as the saying goes, and didn't have any popular music memorized. At my wedding dance in September 1948, John played with the band at the Women's Institute Hall, Beaver Mines.

Behind Bruce Bohne, foreman, in the corral of the Buckhorn Ranch, 1950, is the barn built by George Byron Smith on NE18-5-2-5 in abour 1905 (Map 5). Dave Harder recalled my Dad, Ralph, riding a bronc in this corral. There was quite a steep hill and the bronc bucked uphill. Dad just rolled out of the saddle and down the hill, jumped back up and back got on the bronc. Dave said, "he went right after him again!" Dad was 60 years old. As a 'dude' ranch, the Buckhorn was an integral part of the community.

(Above) Harry and Pearl Zurowski barn on Beaver (Mines) Creek, east of Beaver Mines on NE11-6-2-5 (Map 3). Their brand **"HZ"** is emblazoned in white letters on the barn.

(Left) Harry Zurowski married Pearl Leschuk Mazur in Hillcrest, AB, 1920.

Colin and Mary Ann Currie's barn on Beaver (Mines) Creek, east of Beaver Mines on NE10-6-2-5 (Map 3). When I was a child, their quarter was owned by their son, George.

Colin and Mary Currie were active members of Mountain Mill Church. In 1901, Mary was the first white woman to settle west of Mountain Mill. Colin's sister, Flora, married Adam Stafford of Cowley. Alexander Naismith Mouat, Mary's brother, bought the Butte Ranch on the South Fork of the Oldman River from Fred Godsal. The Butte Ranch originally stretched from Pincher Creek to the Crowsnest Pass. Alexander Mouat gave his original copy of "The History of the Early Days of Pincher Creek" to my Dad.

About 1912, the Pincher Creek Livery, Feed and Sale Barn on Main Street. The barn was built by Fred Robbins, later sold to the Lynch Brothers and burned in 1913. (L to R) John Whittaker, Bill Reid, Harold Vroom and Alf Langton. Used with the kind permission of the Pincher Creek and District Historical Society. Accession Number 994.29.12.

Here about 1915, Uncle Harold Vroom built this barn on his homestead on Beaver (Mines) Creek on SE32-5-2-5 (Map 3). In 2016, it was still in use on my friend Rosalie Biron McLaughlin's ranch. The barn has a flared gambrel or Dutch Colonial roof. Coincidentally, my Vroom family were of Dutch origin. They sailed from the Netherlands in 1638 and settled on Long Island, New York. In 1783, following the American Revolution, they settled in Nova Scotia as United Empire Loyalists.

These barns of upright boards are on the Cecil Dyer ranch, Fir Grove, near Lee Lake. The Dyers were good friends of my family. In about 1937, when I was 10 years old, Dad and I stopped there while driving cattle north to Percy Dennis's in the Maycroft district for winter pasture. It was late fall. Dad and I had started out in the dark and were very cold. Mrs. Bessie Dyer kindly made us a hot meal – a true gesture of Old West hospitality.

On the Herbert Hatfield ranch, Twin Butte district, about 1890, a log barn of dovetail notch construction and chinking, with mud & stick roof. The women are unknown. Used with the kind permission of the Pincher Creek and District Historical Society.

Jim Anderson homestead barn NE16-6-28-4, Halifax district. Jjm and Bessie's daughter, Hazel, married 'Dutch' Truitt of Gladstone Valley, a great friend of my Vroom family. Some settlers from the Halifax to Utopia districts got logs for their buildings from Wood Mtn, a day's travel to the west by team and wagon (Map 5).

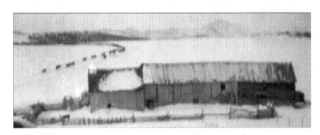

The homestead barn of Fred Clavel on SE36-5-1-5. Here in 1925, it's Alphie Primeau's barn. Summer 1934, I stayed with the Primeau's while Mom was down East for arthritis treatment.

A dry, warm barn housed work and saddle horses in all seasons. This 1970 photo is the *circa* 1930 barn of Frenchy and Nellie Gladstone Riviere, still standing on their Victoria Peak ranch (Map 5). It was made of logs with stalls and mangers, and a few stanchions for milk cows. Long and fairly low, it stabled the Riviere's many saddle horses and withstood the heavy snows in their mountain valley.

About 1907, the barn of the Waterton Oil, Land and Power Co. situated near the sawmill operated by Henry Hanson on the Maskinonge (Maps 1 & 4). The barn housed the horses and oxen which hauled the logs cut at the head of Upper Waterton Lake. The barn was made of milled lumber and stood on the rise at the eastern end of the Waterton River Bridge in 2020. The men are unknown.

Across from Lake Linnet, Waterton, 1922. (Left) 'Pop' Harwood barn, built 1921, and house with post office built 1919. (Centre & right) Barn, bunkhouse and house, built 1921 by J. Bevan & J. Mishico, Guides & Outfitters. The Bevan house was bought by George Annand, Sr, in 1944. George built his garage on the footprint of the Bevan barn. Entrance gate in front of Harwood house built about 1922.

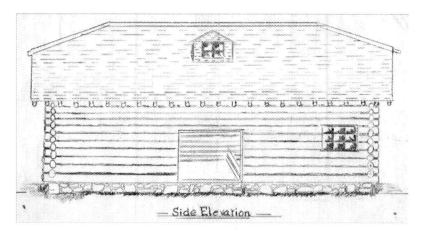

About 1925, this drawing by Walter B. Foster is for the dairy barn of my father-in-law, George Annand, Sr, on Block 16, Lot 6, T1-R30-W4, near the northshore of Middle Waterton Lake  It was the first dairy situated in Waterton. Parks Canada Archives.

Waterton townsite, about 1919. (L to R) Jack Hazzard Tent Camp and Hotel, Dewitt Johnson Garage, Lorin Allred's house and livery stable. Used with the kind permission of the Pincher Creek and District Historical Society.

About 1955, log barn and cookhouse, Headquarters, Waterton. In the 1920s, workhorses pulled the graders and plows that George Annand, Sr, drove. The 'barn boss' was Jack Gladstone.

Chrissie Christiansen and her son, Jack, at the Belly River warden station in 1945. Jack had just returned from overseas with the Canadian Army. (Right) Warden station barn; photo taken looking northeast. Like other Park wardens, Jack's dad, Chris, in the 1930s and 1940s, and Jack in the 1950s, patrolled the Belly River district on horseback. The barn stabled the horses and stored their feed.

In the 1930s. Bert Barnes (left) is loading hay he grew nearby into the loft of the Belly River warden station barn. Bert was a Waterton warden for 23 years. Many wardens had to grow feed for their horses near their station. As well, oats were grown at the north end Stoney Creek Flats. Hay was grown on Pass Creek Flats.

The barn of Lake-Side Saddle Horse Co. was built by brothers Martin & 'Slim' Wacher in 1944 on the site of the former dairy of George Annand, Sr. Here about 1955, it serves Andy Russell's Skyline Saddle Horse Co. In 1957, it becaume Dave Simpson's Timerline Saddle Horses. (Mid-foreground) Wrangler bunkhouse. Credit: John Russell

In the early 1940s, Jack Holroyd is on 'Judy' leading a string of horses. Judy and 'Patches', at the rear, were ridden to Waterton Park School. Patches was given to Jack by James Riviere as an orphan weanling. (Right) The barn and hayloft at Cedar Cabin warden station on Knight's Lake where hay was stored for Holroyd's horses. Hay for other warden horses was stored at the 'Hay Barn' on Pass Creek Flats.

Park View School barn, with simple gable roof, on Cal Wellman's place. The barn was moved from its original location on Klem Pedersen's land NW corner Sec33-2-29-4. Cal owns Klem's homestead brand.

Built in 1914 on NE corner Sec 7-3-29-4, the Spread Eagle School and barn were moved in 1926 by a team of 32 horses to SW corner Sec 30-3-30-4. The barn's 'saltbox' roof connects to the shed on the left. The school was sold to the Spread Eagle Community Organization.

Ranchers commonly repurposed buildings for other uses. Built of logs, the first Lee School (Monkey Coulee School) was built in 1898 (#469). In 1911 the School Trustees decided on a new location for the 2nd Lee School. In 1912, the first school was disassembled, log by log, and reassembled on SW4-8-2-5 as Albert Connelly, Sr's horse barn, as shown here. The barn is still in use in 2021.

(Left) Here about 1914, the middle portion of this barn was built as the LDS Meeting House, Caldwell, AB, when Geo and Betsy Annand worked on the Bradshaw-Jacobs Ranch. It became the LDS Tithing Barn. Then, with lean-to additions, it became Jim Jacobs' barn. The unknown cowboy, on his handsome horse, is wearing a fringed buckskin jacket with bead embroidery.

(Right) Archie Vroom homestead cabin and barn about 1911. On NW 35-5-2-5, Archie built the homestead house and barn so he could live there while building the 'Archie Vroom' School. This cabin became Dad's carpenter shop. The barn became our goat house where I spend many happy hours as a child playing with my beloved goats.

The chicken coop on my Uncle Harold Vroom homestad in the Beaver (Mines) Creek Valley, had several lives (Map 3). First, the coop (left wing) was become the 'Chicken Coop' School from 1939-1941 (Cathie Bower, teacher). Here, about 1942, the school house entry porch has been enlarged to 2-storeys and the right wing added as quarters for tourists who came from back East to tour Western Canada.

In 1880, the Dept. of Indian Affairs built Farm #23, 'Indian Farm' beside Indianfarm (Chipman) Creek on N½34-5-4. It was a failure in training the Peigan to farm. They planted potatoes by day and dug them up for food at night. About 1882, the NWMP used the farm to grow feed for their horses. To keep the buffalo out of the field, deep, wide furrows were plowed around the field; buffalo would not cross soft ground. This NWMP log barn was one of two built. Ben Harder, Sr. is in his barnyard in 1942.

This log barn is what remained of one of the two barns built by NWMP on their 'Indian Farm'. Built on N½-34-5-4, this dilapidated barn was taken apart and moved by Ernie Brown to his farm, which is the location shown in this 1970 photo.

But, what if there is no barn for refuge? During the night of September 11, 2017, a wall of fire swept from Sage Pass and down Pass Creek Valley. The Kenow Fire consumed the Waterton buffalo paddocks and roared out into the Park View district. Days earlier, the Waterton buffalo herd had been transported to Grasslands NP, SK.

That is, all except one recalcitrant old bull who refused to be corralled. Park wardens assumed the bull had been killed in the ensuing conflagration. But the next day, the bull was found safe and sound. He'd taken refuge by stnading in a small lake in the summer paddock. As his ancestors for millennia before him, the bull knew how to survive a prairie fire.

# LONG TRAIL A-WINDING

♫ ♫ There's a long, long trail a-winding, Into the land of my dreams, And I know I'll ride there someday, In the sweet bye and bye. ♫ ♫

A-kwote-kátl-nam (Kootenai or Chief Mountain) Lake; 1860 watercolour by James Alden, artist for the Boundary Commission. The survey party had slashed a trail along the 49th parallel from the West Kootenays. Four teepees stand at the Narrows. Bert Colclough (born 1890) said when he was a child an old Indian said at one time these lakes harboured fish 'as big as a horse'. Were these sturgeons which took refuge at the end of the last ice age? National Archives, Washington 305550/76-E221-ALDEN66

Travois Trail on Sofa Mtn, Waterton (Map 4). The ruts of travois poles were still visible on Stoney Creek Flats in the 1960s. Kootenai Brown recalled an 1878 tragedy that claimed the lives of three Kootenais. A man and two women went up Sofa to hunt mountain sheep. They were caught in a blizzard above the tree line. They froze to death, the women with the sheep's skin covering their heads. Since Kootenai (Kutenai) were a 'mountain' tribe, it was very unusal for them to be caught like this. A loose rock cairn covering their bodies still stood on the far side of Sofa Mtn in the 1940s. (Right) Sheep Mtn, now Vimy Ridge.

View southwest from Pine Ridge on Hwy 6. (Far left) Chief Mtn to the Waterton Valley (far right). A mile-long line of Stoney men, women and children, annually followed the Old North (Sundance, Stoney Indian) Trail across the Kootenai (Waterton) River. They wound their way south past Chief Mtn to the Sundance in Montana. (Foreground) Cottonwood Creek Flat where Cal Wellman found stones of 17 teepee rings.

Hugh Dempsey told me that William S. Lee likely arrived north of the Medicine Line in 1872. This is the site of Lee's trading post located one mile southwest of Beazer, AB. Lee built here because it was a main camp area for the Stoneys on their way to the Montana Sundance. This was on Lee Creek, which flows through Cardston. In the mid-1870s, Lee moved to the Pincher Creek area. Lee Lake is named forr him. Lee's brand was '41', later sold to A.H. and R. Lynch-Staunton.

(Left) North Fork Belly River (flowing east) empties into the Belly River (flowing north). The Rivers meet at Beebe Flats named for Joe Beebe, Sr. The remains of Joe's cabin and barn still stood in the 1930s. Joe came from Utah to drive bull teams for I.G. Baker & Co. In 1880 he met Percy Creighton in Fort Macleod. The men cut logs on the (later) Blood Timber Limit 148A, floating them down the Belly River to built homes for settlers. A hunting trail which branched off the Old North Trail followed the Belly River. (Right) Sofa Mtn, Waterton Park. W.C. Alden, U.S. Geological Survey awc00641.

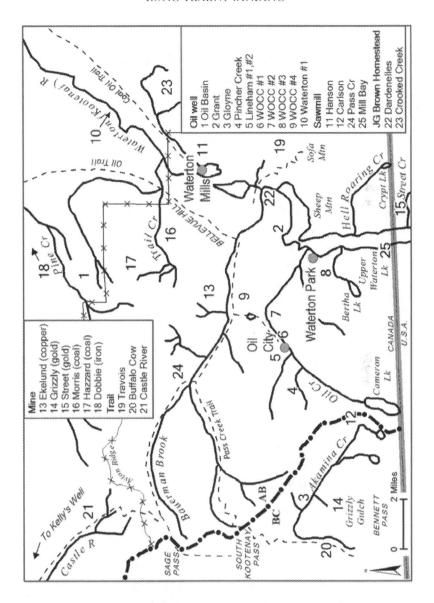

**MAP 4  MINES, OIL WELLS, SAWMILLS, WATERTON PARK, circa 1875-1940**
**Kootenai Brown homesteads:** Crooked Creek, Pass Creek (Dardenelles) **Oil well:**
Gloyne Akamina #1, Grant's Imperial Oil, Lineham #1 & #2, Oil Basin, Pincher Creek
Oil & Refining Co, Western Oil & Coal Co #1 (Oil City). WOCC #2 (Cameron Bend),
WOCC #3 (Waterton townsite), WOCC #4 (Pass Creek) **Mine:** William Dobbie, Nels
Ekelund, Grizzly Gulch, Jack Hazzard, Morris Bros., Jack Street **Sawmill:** Henry
Hanson, Carlson, Mill Bay, Pass Creek **Other:** Akamina Creek, Bennett Pass **Trail:**
Buffalo (Cow), Castle River, Travois.

Until the first bridge was built, the Coal Oil Trail from Waterton crossed the shallow 'narrows' at the mouth of Maskinonge Lake where it meets the Waterton River. The trail went eastward from Fred Kanouse's ranch on Lower Waterton Lake, then north across the 'narrows' (shown here), and onward northeast to Fort Macleod (Map 1).

(Left) NW from Crandell (Bear) Mtn, 1914. Oil Trail wends its way (from upper left, down right side of photo) across the Badlands to Oil City. For 50 miles, horses pulled heavy freight wagons loaded with boilers and drilling equipment from Pincher City to oil wells in Pass Creek Valley and Oil (Cameron) Creek Valley. They forded Drywood and Yarrow Creeks. Finally, they crossed Pass Creek at the bottom right of (far left) Bellevue Hill where the ruts of the wagon wheels can be seen in 2021 (Maps 1 & 4). Credit: M.P. Bridgland 1914/Geodetic Survey /Library and Archives Canada / e002107347

(Right) View north from Cameronian Mtn (Buchanan Ridge) at Cameron Bend to Pass Creek Valley, 1914. The point where Oil Trail crossed at the ford over Pass Creek (lower middle, photo above) was also the location of the bull pasture fence used by local ranchers.

(Right) Oil Trail ran west, up the south side of Pass Creek until it was parallel with Blue (Crandell) Lake. The final drop into the Cameron Creek Valley (bottom foreground) was so precipitous that wagons were winched. The trail is visible in the lower left where it ran directly south, past the west side of Blue Lake (Map 4). M.P. Bridgland 1914/Geodetic Survey /Library and Archives Canada / e002108101

Visible on the far left is the trail used in 1902 by George Stewart of the Drywood district to haul supplies by pack horse to the oil wells in Waterton townsite and on to Oil City. Here in 1919, the trail runs up the hill from Lake Linnet, across the moraine where the Prince of Wales stands in 2021 and down into the town. It was a lonely, arduous 3-day round trip. George often visited with Kootenai Brown and Nichemoos at their Pass Creek homestead and stayed in the Bill Aldridge log cabin at Lake Linnet.

About 1935, view northwest, the bridge built over Red Rock Canyon to connect the trails up Pass Creek Valley and to Sage Pass and the Castle River Valley (Map 4) (Centre) Lester 'Mac' McAllister, Park warden. (Right) Waddy Foster flourishing a hatchet. (Back) Riviere Bros. saddle horse rentals. The tents are in the same location as my Vroom family's horse rentals the summers of 1940 and 1941.

Fall 1947, Bob Thomas on 'Baldy' atop Sage Pass, viewing southwest to Glacier National Park (Maps 4 & 5). Bob said Baldy could go through brush "at 100 mph" and never bump your knee! Bob was a wrangler for Andy Russell on a big game hunting trip. 'Pop' Harwood was cook. Once they crossed into BC, they required Levi Ashman as a licensed BC Guide. The party travelled three weeks, going down Kishenina Creek to the Flathead Valley and back, ending at Wall Lake. It was a hunting route previously used by Bert Riggall.

(L to R) Don Vroom (son of Ralph), Vera Gingras (daughter of Marion), Marion Cyr and Ralph Vroom (siblings). In 1968, they're standing on the old site of Kelly's Wells at the north end of the Castle River Valley. This is on the trail from Beaver Mines, up the Castle River, over Avion Ridge (Castle Divide) and into Waterton Park, a trail they all had ridden in younger days.

This family post card shows Castle Turret (Castle Peak) on renamed Windsor Mountain (Map 5). From the east the cliffs of the mountain look very challenging. However, the west side is a safe, strenuous, climb. In my book, *The Vrooms of the Foothills: Volume 1, Adventures of My Childhood*, is a description of my experience climbing to the base of this tower in 1938, when I was 11 years old. Guided by my Dad, I climbed it along with my cousin Vera Cyr (Gingras) of Pincher Creek, and my brothers, Don and Bill.

Snowslide Meadow ranger station (cache), Dominion Forestry Branch, at the head of the Castle River, 1922. It was below Big Horn Pass and Avion Ridge (Castle Divide) (Map 5). Located 23 miles south of the Castlemount ranger station, it was on the forest ranger patrol trails coming from Bovin (Blue) Lake, North and South Yarrow Creek and Red Rock Canyon (Castle River Trail).

In 2007, Gerry Annand is gazing northward, down the Castle River Valley from Avion Ridge. The Valley is more beautiful here than the summer of '36 when a raging forest fire burned up the grizzly bears' natural food supply. It caused starving grizzlies to go outside the Forest Reserve and kill nearby ranchers' cattle. In 1936, I rode with my Dad and stock rider Pete LaGrandeur to a point on the right side of the Valley when Dad went to get the grizzly bear out of the trap he'd set (Maps 4 & 5). It was an exciting adventure that I describe in *Volume 1, Adventures of My Childhood*.

Bert Riggall's pack train, on a shale slope similar to Avion Ridge. Taking horses from Avion Ridge (Castle Divide) down to Goat Lake, is unwise. It's safer to use the descent on the west end of the Ridge down to Bauerman Brook. (Maps 4 & 5).

In 1935, we stayed with Scottie Morris in his house, second from left on Middle Waterton Lake. In August 1938, my Dad, my brother Don, Aileen Lunn, Blanche Pope and I (11 years old) travelled for 10 days by pack and saddle horses from our ranch at Beaver Mines up the Castle River, over the Castle Divide Trail (Avion Ridge) and down Pass Creek Valley to Waterton townsite (Map 4 & 5). It was a memorable trip. I loved trail riding, camping, and just riding my favourite horse. On the return to Beaver Mines, we followed the forest ranger Boundary Trail along the east edge of the mountains.

View west to Butcher Lake, near the junction of Boundary and Pincher Creek Trails (Map 5). It's named for Harold Butcher, homestead NW16-4-30-4. (Mid-back) Victoria Peak. The Pincher Creek Trail was dead end.

'Lord' Brooke's hunting cabin on upper Pincher Creek. It was used as a cabin (cache) by Dominion forest rangers when patrolling the Boundary and Pincher Creek Trails (Map 5). Here in the early 1950s, it is Frenchy Riviere's 'little log cabin in the woods'.

(L to R) Charlie and James Riviere on Big Horn Pass at the junction of three forest ranger patrol trails - South and North Yarrow Creek and Bovin (Blue) Lake (Map 5). They're heading out on a hunting trip. Viewing northwest down the Castle River Valley, Snowslide Meadow cabin (cache) is just below the left side of this early 1930s photo.

**MAP 5 CASTLE RIVER FOREST RESERVE, circa 1905-1945. Forest ranger cabin/cache:** Brooke, Castlemount (Castle River), Elk Lodge, Forks, Lynx Creek, Mill Creek, Snowslide Meadow, Yarrow **Homestead/ranch:** Andy Bower, Buckhorn, Henri 'Fenchy' Riviere, Harold Vroom, Ralph Vroom, Oscar Vroom, Alex Wells **Trail:** Boundary, Bovin (Blue) Lake, Castle River, South, Middle & North Kootenay, North Yarrow, South Yarrow **Oil well:** Canadian North-West Oil #1, #2, #3 and #4, Kelly's wells **Creek, river, lake:** Bauerman Brook, Beaver (Mines) Creek, Beaver Mines Lake, Carbondale (Railway) River, Castle River (South Fork of Oldman), Kishenina Creek, Lynx Creek, Mill Creek, North Yarow (Smith) Creek, Pincher Creek, South Drywood (Carpenter) Creek, South Yarrow Creek, West Castle River, **Other:** Carbondale townsite, Carbon Hill fire lookout, Castle Turret, Corner Mtn (Wood Mtn, Prairie Bluff), Gladstone Valley, Petroleum (Barnaby) Ridge, Table Mtn, Victoria Peak, Waterton Park, Windsor Mtn.

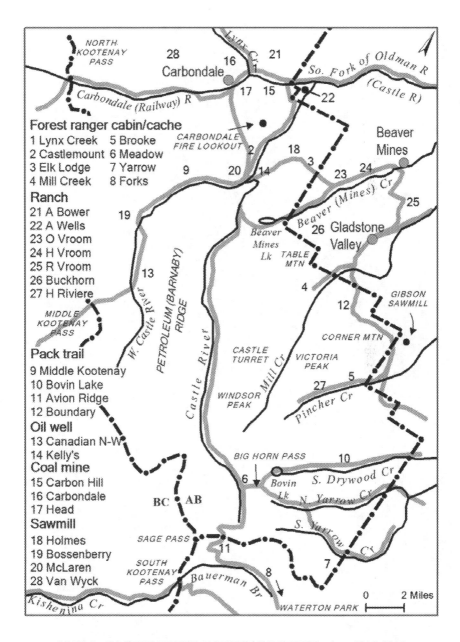

**MAP 5   CASTLE RIVER FOREST RESERVE, circa 1900-1945**
(continued) **Coal mine:**  Carbondale, Carbon Hill Coal & Coke, Head Syndicate Ltd
**Sawmill:**  Bossenberry #2, Gibson, Holmes (Bossenberry #1), McLaren, Van Wcyk
**Mountain Pass:**  Avion Ridge (Castle Divide), Big Horn, Middle Kootenay, North
Kootenay, Sage, South Kootenay.

1883, Dominion Survey party at the summit of North Kootenay Pass (Map 5). In 1875, John Shaw drove a herd of cattle over this pass from the Tobacco Plains, BC, to Morley, NWT. Capt. Palliser said this was the route for a railway to BC. Instead the Crowsnest Pass was chosen. Credit: Library and Archives Canada / PA-050760

(L to R) Bob Sharp, Charlie Page, George Hassett at Mill Creek ranger station. About 1930, a rotary rig was brought to the Mount Royal #1, SE of Mountain Mill. Dave Harder said Bob Sharp subsequently took 1000 feet of cable from the old rig over the North Kootenay Pass to the Sage Creek seeps. The continuous cable was looped around pack saddles on a string of mules (Map 1).

In June 1914, my dad, Ralph Vroom, stands partially visible on the far left. On the reverse Dad wrote "My pack string on east side of Middle Kootenay Pass. There was 50 feet of snow on 7th June." The fishing party was on their way to Flathead country. Dad's dog, Jock, is laying on the packhorse at left (Map 5).

# EPILOGUE

My next book, my sixth in the series *The Vrooms of the Foothills*, will be a lot of fun. There will be photos of parades and community activities, automobiles, children and their school ponies, sawmills, forest rangers and homes.

Dominion Day parade, Pincher Creek, 1927, turning west on Main Street.. (L to R) McRobert's Dept. Store, Montgomery & Hart Garage, Betterway Grocery Store, Cadillac Café and the Scott Block. Over the NW corner of the M & H Garage is the flag on the firehall. Pincher Creek High School occupied the second floor of this building.

1913 (L to R) Wessano and Islay Huddlestun, and unknown baby in Lu Nielson's Ford Model T in Waterton. The girls were the daughters of Billy Huddlestun.

Bessie Vroom on Pickles after a spring weekend visiting Granny Mary Tyson in Utopia district, 1942. I'm carrying my box of clothes and riding to Wes Thomas' to get a lift back to the Pincher Creek High School dormitory along with his daughters, Jean and Shirley.

About 1927, George Riviere in his lean-to on hhis traplime. He and his brother, Henri, Jr, had traplines on the Kishenina and Sage Creeks just west of Waterton Park. Along with working for local ranchers, they made extra money trapping beavers, muskrats and marten.

All Saints Anglican Church, Waterton Park, on September 30, 1928. Inscribed on the reverse: *"The First Harvest Thanksgiving, All Saints Church, Waterton Park, Sept 30th, 1928. Service by Rev. Canon Middleton. From his Warden, A.H. Harwood".*

One of two illuminated manuscripts with names of Waterton residents, many members of All Saints Church, "WHO VOLUNTEERED FOR ACTIVE SERVICE WITH CANADA'S FIGHTING FORCES" in WW2.

(In alphabetical order) Henry Levern 'Vern' Albiston, Levi Ashman (also enlisted in WW1), Robert Ayris, George 'Geordie' Annand, Reginald E.F. Bailey, Gordon W Bell, Alton 'Hoot' Carlson, Ethel Carnell, Jean Carnell, Raymond 'Ray' Carnell, Jack Christiansen, Edwin Cummings, Tom Delany, Cameron Dickson, Robert Dickson, Delton Ellison, Arthur Frederickson, Vern Gairns, Clinton R. Goble, Ed Goble, Frank Goble, Kevin Goble, William Gregory, Arthur Holroyd, Douglas Matkin, Roy McKenzie, Donald Morris, Charles Nixon, Howard Peterson, Bert Pittaway, Dennis Pittaway, John Pittaway, Kay Rackette, C. Schweitzer, E.D. Schweitzer, Victor Stewart, L. Dee Strate, Sheldon Strate, Robert Taylor, Clarke Tourond, David Tourond (also enlisted in WW1), Fred A.G. Udell, Ralph Vroom (also enlisted in WW1), William Ralph Webb, John Wellman, Harry Wellman, Kenneth Williams, Pete Woolf, Victor Woolf.

# MAPS

About 1911, (L to R) Robert Gladstone, Albert Dumont, Charley Smith and Kootenai Brown. Robert was a ranger in the Castle River Forest Reserve. Albert rode for the McLaren Ranch at Mountain Mill. Charley's Metis wife, Marie Rose, wrote the historic series "Eighty Years on the Plains" for the Canadian Cattlemen magazine.

Beaver Mines Women's Instisute, 1933, with attendees gathering in the WI Hall to make a quilt. The WI, to which my mother Mollie Vroom belonged, met once a month to engage rural women in educational and community endeavours. (L to R) Lettie Lowery, Vice-President, Edna McDonald, Treasurer, Emma McDowall, Sarah Ballantyne, Secretary, Jessie Hamilton, President and Annie Ruby Bainbridge.

(Left) In Waterton Park townsite at Western Oil & Coal Company #4 oil well on (now) Evergreen Ave near Cameron Falls, 1911 (Map 4). The view is to the west up Oil (Cameron) Creek. (L to R) Palmer Stafford and unknown men. Palmer and his son, George, came from Ontario to drill in Waterton. Later, George was a driller at Weymarn Oils #1 at Mountain Mill. Photo by A. Knechtel, 1911. Dominion Forestry Branch, Alberta: Alberta Forest Service Collection.

(Below) Hanson Sawmill building a dam for logging at the head of Upper Waterton Lake, about 1907. The men are unknown. 'Buck and 'Bride' are the only working oxen the Hanson's owned. John Hanson recalled as a boy riding behind the team.

In 1962, unknown men on a tour inspect the capped drill stem of the original Discovery #1 oil well, Oil City, Waterton (Map 4). They're waiting for commentary from Lethbridge historian, Wilbur McKenzie.

# REFERENCES

Bruce-Brooks, A. Circa 1994. Dad's Memories. Happy 80th Birthday Dad! Unpublished.

Djuff, R. 1999. High on a Windy Hill: The Story of the Prince of Wales Hotel. Published by Rocky Mountain Books, Calgary, AB

Blairmore Enterprise. 1939 August 4: "The Castle River Club's Annual Stampede"

BC Historical News. February 1975. Vol 8. No. 2. "A Traverse of East Kootenay Survey History" by G.S. Andrews

Canadian Oil and Gas Industries. 1955. Vol 8. No 8. 'Oil Pioneers of Western Canada'

Colclough, A. and F.H. Schofield. 1980. Pincher Papers. Published by the Pincher Creek and District Historical Society and Local History New Horizons Project, Pincher Creek, AB

Crowsnest and Its People. 1979. Published by Crowsnest Pass Historical Society, Coleman, AB

Dormaar, J.F. and Watt, R.A. 2007. Oil City: black gold in Waterton Park. Occasional Paper No. 45 of The Lethbridge Historical Society. City of Lethbridge, Lethbridge, AB

Forget, S. 1991. Beauvais School, A Collected and Living History. University of Lethbridge, Faculty of Education. In partial fulfillment of the requirements for the degree of tMaster of Education.

Getty, I.A.L. 1971. A History of the Human Settlement at Waterton Lakes National Park, 1800-1937. A research paper prepared for the National and Historic Parks Branch, Department of Indian Affairs and Northern Development, Ottawa, ON

Goble, Frank. Privately published by Goble Publishing Ltd., Cardston, AB
- 1996. The Trapper, Volume 1
- 1998. The Trapper, Volume 3
- 2003. Trails Growed Over, Book 1, The Pioneers

Huddlestun, F.A. Circa 1969. A History of the Settlement and Building Up of the Area in S.W. Alberta Bordering Waterton Park on the North From 1889. Privately published

Knox, E. 2015. Cal Wellman Oral History Interview. Parks Canada. Waterton Lakes National Park. Unpublished manuscript

The Lethbridge Herald.
- 1928 May 26. Pg 7. 'The Lone Survivor at Kootenai Brown's Table' by J. C. Cosley
- 1929 June 22. Pg 4. 'The Temperment of Kootenai Brown' by Joseph C. Cosley

- 1954 June 28. 'Biggest Day in Park's History: Rain Fails to Dampen Waterton Day as Over 10000 Visitors Jam Park'
- 1957 Oct 5. Page 18. 'Growth of Waterton Park', by Mrs. Bessie M. Annand

Lynch-Staunton, E. Circa 1920. A History of the Early Days of Pincher Creek: of the District and of the Southern Mountains. Published by the Members of the Women's Institute of Alberta

Mather, K. 2013. Frontier Cowboys and the Great Divide: Early Ranching in BC and Alberta. Heritage House Publishing Company Ltd., Victoria, BC

Middleton, S. (pseudonym 'Chief Mountain'). 1954. Kootenai Brown: Adventurer... Pioneer... Plainsman...Park Warden and Waterton Lakes National Park. Lethbridge, AB: Lethbridge Herald Job Department

Morrison, C. 2008. Waterton Chronicles: People and Their National Park. Published by Goathaunt Publishing, Lethbridge, AB

Nelson, J. M. 1967. Mountain View Remembers. Privately published, Mountain View, AB

Pincher Creek and District Historical Society. 1974. Prairie grass to mountain pass. History of the Pioneers of Pincher Creek and District. Published by Pincher Creek and District Historical Society

Pincher Creek and District Historical Society. 2013. Prairie Grass to Mountain Pass: History of the Pioneers of Pincher Creek and District. Published by Pincher Creek and District Historical Society

Pincher Creek and District School Division #29. 1992. Unfolding the Pages. Printed by Pincher Creek Echo, Alberta

Pincher Creek Echo. 2007 Apr 20. "The Evolution of Gas and Oil Exploration in the 1920s" by Farley Wuth

Tait, W. M., "I Remember", Recollections of Kootenai Brown, Rrelated Verbatim to W.M.T., Copied from the Farm and Ranch Review, Vols. 15-16, Calgary, 1919-1920

Western People. 1984 Aug 16. "Wild Men", by Gray Campbell

# INDEX

# INDEX

INDEX

# ABOUT THE AUTHOR

Bessie Vroom Ellis attended one-room country schools for her elementary grades, riding on horseback and making a round trip of nearly nine miles each day. She graduated from Pincher Creek High School and attended Calgary Normal School. Along with 120 other students Ms. Ellis graduated with a Wartime Emergency Certificate in Elementary Education; she started teaching in a country school on January 3, 1945. When she first taught at Waterton Park School in 1947-48, Ms. Ellis met, and then married, local resident Geordie Annand They raised a family of four children.

During her more than 20 years in Waterton Park, the author honed her writing skills. She wrote feature articles, and a thrice-weekly column called 'Wonderful Waterton', for *The Lethbridge Herald*. As well, Ms. Ellis contributed news items to three other newspapers, two in Calgary and one in Montana, and to CJOC Radio and CJLH-TV in Lethbridge, AB. She was active in the Girl Guides of Canada and in the Anglican Church of Canada.

After 15 years the author returned to her teaching career, updating her qualifications through night extension classes, Summer School and day classes. She was awarded a Bachelor of Education degree by the University of Lethbridge and a Master of Education degree by University of Alberta, and then taught in Lethbridge, AB. After her remarriage in 1975 Ms. Ellis moved to Regina, SK, teaching there for another 15 years for a total of over 29 years of service in the teaching profession. In Regina she earned a post-graduate Diploma in Educational Administration from the University of Regina.

During her years in Regina the author travelled extensively. She was active in politics, running for office herself and then working to promote the election of more women at the provincial and federal levels. In the early 1980s the Saskatchewan New Democratic Women (SNDW) established the Bessie Ellis Fund to assist women running for nomination.

In 1992, Ms. Ellis was awarded the Commemorative Medal for the 125th Anniversary of the Confederation of Canada, 1867-1992, "in recognition of significant contribution to compatriots, community and to Canada." Upon retirement Ms. Ellis returned to her writing.

Printed in the United States
by Baker & Taylor Publisher Services